on track ...
The
Damned

every album, every song

Morgan Brown

sonicbondpublishing.com

Sonicbond Publishing Limited
www.sonicbondpublishing.co.uk
Email: info@sonicbondpublishing.co.uk

First Published in the United Kingdom 2021
First Published in the United States 2021

British Library Cataloguing in Publication Data:
A Catalogue record for this book is available from the British Library

Copyright Morgan Brown 2021

ISBN 978-1-78952-136-8

Typeset in ITC Garamond & ITC Avant Garde
Printed and bound in England

Graphic design and typesetting: Full Moon Media

This book is dedicated to Stef Bradley, without whose support, patience and encouragement I could never have started, let alone completed this project.

I would like to thank Stephen Lambe of Sonicbond Publishing for giving me the opportunity to write this book, cheerfully tolerating my general cluelessness, and providing this first-time author with a wealth of much-needed guidance. I also owe a debt of gratitude to Paul Abbott, whose peerless research skills provided me with the true story behind 'Under The Floor Again'. Finally, I'd like to express my gratitude to all members of The Damned, past and present, for nearly half a century of astonishing music. May you keep walking that street of dreams for many years to come.

Would you like to write for Sonicbond Publishing?

We are mainly a music publisher, but we also occasionally publish in other genres including film and television. At Sonicbond Publishing we are always on the look-out for authors, particularly for our two main series, On Track and Decades.

Mixing fact with in depth analysis, the On Track series examines the entire recorded work of a particular musical artist or group. All genres are considered from easy listening and jazz to 60s soul to 90s pop, via rock and metal.

The Decades series singles out a particular decade in an artist or group's history and focuses on that decade in more detail than may be allowed in the On Track series.

While professional writing experience would, of course, be an advantage, the most important qualification is to have real enthusiasm and knowledge of your subject. First-time authors are welcomed, but the ability to write well in English is essential.

Sonicbond Publishing has distribution throughout Europe and North America, and all our books are also published in E-book form. Authors will be paid a royalty based on sales of their book. Further details about our books are available from www.sonicbondpublishing.com. To contact us, complete the contact form there or email info@sonicbondpublishing.co.uk *on track ...*

The Damned

Contents

Introduction

Now we're gonna dance to a different song…

The Damned are one of the most unfairly under-appreciated bands in rock history. Their pioneering efforts paved the way for much of the punk, indie and gothic rock to have emerged internationally over the past forty-plus years, producing a diverse and fascinating body of work, which reveals them to be one of the UK's most enduringly creative bands. And yet, they rarely feature in critics' lists of best albums or most important acts and are often reduced to little more than a footnote in punk rock discussions, while some of their notable contemporaries are regarded as serious art and afforded the according critical respect. While major-label acts, Sex Pistols and The Clash, led by their svengali managers, each presented a simple, bold and marketable image to the world – the Pistols as the shocking, spiky-haired nihilist urchins, The Clash as the socially conscious, culturally-aware rebel rockers – The Damned were a slightly more complex proposition; a mismatched group of characters, more difficult for the various small independent labels to package and promote. The band's longevity has also, paradoxically, been a barrier to their acceptance into the broader rock canon. Whilst The Clash and (especially) the Pistols came and went in a blaze of glory, leaving behind a small but iconic body of work, The Damned's fascinating – if haphazard – career path has created a sprawling, multi-faceted legacy that's been difficult to pin down. Different groups of fans have their preferred version of the group, with some swearing by the raw punk assault of the band's first two albums, some favouring the wider-ranging 1980s expansion into pop and psychedelia, and others remaining devoted to the slickly-packaged gothic Damned who found commercial success in that decade's latter half.

Whether or not critics ever get to grips with the band's complex history, even a cursory study of their back catalogue reveals a veritable treasure trove of exciting and wildly inventive music, created by a revolving cast of unforgettable characters; a band who played a crucial role in punk's development as both a musical style and identity and then shrugged off the straitjacket of that genre's trappings, to follow an idiosyncratic artistic path, often completely oblivious to contemporary trends or critical and commercial expectations.

The initial band line-up came together in 1976, emerging from London's small, incestuous early proto-punk scene. Guitarist, Brian James (who changed his surname from Robertson to avoid being confused with the Thin Lizzy axeman) had been making loud, raw rock 'n' roll in the mould of The Stooges and MC5 for some years, notably with the charmingly-named Brussels-based combo, Bastard, before an advertisement in the *Melody Maker* led him to London SS – a glam/punk outfit in the New York Dolls vein – which also featured Mick Jones (later of The Clash), and Tony James who would go on to form Generation X. Completing the line-up was a wild, energetic drummer named Christopher Millar: soon to be christened Rat Scabies, after the vermin that populated the band's practice space and the skin condition from which he suffered. London SS never got beyond the rehearsal stage, but James and Scabies had formed a significant musical bond.

Following the dissolution of London SS, Rat found his way into a new band being assembled by Sex Pistols manager Malcolm McLaren, which included future Pretenders frontwoman Chrissie Hynde on guitar, and was tentatively dubbed Masters of the Backside! In need of a bassist, Rat suggested one Ray Burns: a toilet cleaner and aspiring musician whom Scabies had befriended during a brief stint working at Croydon's Fairfield Hall. With his long, curly locks shorn, Burns' propensity for madcap recklessness soon earned him an ironic nickname, which became a whole new persona: Captain Sensible. McLaren's concept was for the band to have two singers – one blonde and dressed entirely in white, the other with black hair and clad head to toe in black. The former was a hairdresser named Dave White, who exited show business after the inevitable demise of the Masters of the Backside. The latter was David Lett: an aspiring artist then working as a gravedigger, whose love of classic horror movies and the glamour of Hollywood's golden age had inspired his formal, monochrome style – highly unusual in the gaudy 1970s when black clothing was generally reserved for funerals.

McLaren renamed Lett 'Dave Zero', which fell off once the band fizzled out without playing a gig. However, when asked to sing in James, Scabies and Sensible's new project (after Sid Vicious – who was also invited to audition – failed to turn up), Lett picked a new name for himself: Vanian (as in Transylvanian) – the perfect match for his vampiric demeanour. With the line-up in place, the band named themselves The Damned (possibly after Luchino Visconti's 1969 film of the same name, or perhaps in reference to Wolf Rilla's *Village of the Damned* (1960): an adaptation of John Wyndham's *The Midwich Cuckoos*), and with Brian James acting as *de facto* leader and principal songwriter, they played their first gig on 6 July 1976 at London's 100 Club, supporting Sex Pistols.

Over forty years later, the band have been through numerous incarnations exploring different musical directions, with quite a roll-call of musicians passing through their ranks. Yet somehow, with the vast majority of their contemporaries either long since split up or having accepted the easy money of the nostalgia circuit, The Damned remain a creative force, still producing new music, evolving artistically, and playing to crowds now encompassing several generations. As Dave Vanian told *GQ* magazine in 2019: 'I think the best is yet to come. There's a lot of things I still want to attempt. I never think, 'Oh, I've done it now, I can just sit back and play 'New Rose''''.

Even so, while a handful of The Damned's songs have passed into the broader mainstream consciousness, most accounts of the band tend to focus largely on the more outrageous aspects of their personalities and their legendary debauchery and bad behaviour, with little serious attention paid to their hugely impressive body of work. Hopefully, this book will serve as a small step towards redressing that injustice and establishing The Damned as one of the truly great British rock bands, and not just a punk footnote.

Damned Damned Damned (1977)

Personnel:
Dave Vanian: vocals
Brian James: guitar, vocals
Captain Sensible: bass, vocals
Rat Scabies: drums, vocals
Producer: Nick Lowe
Engineer: Bazza (Barry Farmer)
Recorded at Pathway Studios, London
Record label: Stiff Records
Release date: 18 February 1977 (UK), 16 April 1977 (US)
Highest chart position: UK: 36
Running time: 31:32
Current edition: 2017 BMG Records CD/LP

Even if the Damned had never released another LP – a scenario which probably seemed entirely plausible to the band themselves at the time – 1977's *Damned Damned Damned* would be more than enough to secure their place in the rock pantheon. The very first UK punk LP, in a mere 31 breathless minutes it captured the power, vibrancy, attitude and sheer fun of this new music. Furthermore, for all the band's chaotic slapstick nihilism and deliberately trashy aesthetic, there was real musical substance here: timeless rock 'n' roll played with an urgency and skill that suggested there might be more to punk than the 'gobbing and safety pins' image which Malcolm McLaren had gleefully cultivated, and the tabloid press had eagerly lapped.

Preceding the LP – in October 1976 – The Damned's debut single (and the first single by a UK punk band) 'New Rose' was a short, sharp cocktail of primal power chords, raging hormones and amphetamine frenzy, which was about as striking an opening statement as any band ever made. The effect was compounded on the B-side: a joyful ransacking of the Beatles classic, 'Help', transforming the original's easy swing into a freewheeling speed-freak cacophony. This wilfully sacrilegious (if in this case, not entirely unaffectionate) treatment of the previous generation's established idols was to become something of a calling card for the first wave of British punk rockers, with many recording their own withering covers of pop classics, in order to thumb their noses at the old guard; as The Clash sang: 'No Elvis, Beatles or The Rolling Stones, in 1977'.

Like the 'New Rose' single, *Damned Damned Damned* was produced by fellow Stiff Records alumnus, Nick Lowe: a veteran of the London pub rock circuit as a member of Brinsley Schwartz. It is quite probable that primarily, convenience and cost considerations motivated the choice of Lowe as producer. Indie label Stiff, could not offer the lavish budgets afforded to some of The Damned's major label contemporaries, and getting the album finished quickly and with a minimum of fuss, was definitely a priority. However, whatever the initial reasoning, Lowe's appointment turned out to be an inspired choice. Although his own records are generally immaculately crafted polished power pop gems, here Lowe captures the fury and spontaneity of the early Damned to perfection, leaving all rough edges fully intact, channelling the sound into a fiercely-compressed midrange roar which tears out of your speakers. A sleeve instruction notes that the LP is 'Made to be played loud at low volume', and sure enough, even at neighbour-friendly levels, there's still a thrilling sensation of everything edging into the red on the mixing desk, and everyone clamouring to be heard through the glorious din. Unlike most modern rock records, there's precious little separation between instruments and few overdubs; Vanian's vocals are double-tracked throughout, and James is allowed a second guitar track so he can add some rhythm chords to underpin his leads, but that's it. It creates the impression that you're listening to a very loud band playing live in a very small room, and it's thoroughly exhilarating. As Sensible says: 'It would have been a tragedy to overproduce it. It sounds raw and rancid and gnarled. To spruce it up would have been a mistake'.

Ever since the Ramones first stood against a brick wall, looking surly in leather jackets and ripped jeans, the 'band as a gang' image has been *de rigueur* for punk groups. Indeed since the early days of rock, it's been standard behaviour for bands to present themselves with a unified style and attitude. Not so for The Damned. From day one, it was clear that this was a group of four quite distinct personalities, none of whom were willing to compromise in any way to fit in any better with the other three, and the sleeve of their debut LP captures this perfectly. The front cover image was taken by Peter Kodick, who had the inspired idea of staging a custard pie fight for the shoot. The used shot shows the four band members just after all the pies have flown, and immediately reveals something about each personality: Captain Sensible, particularly layered with goo, smiles benignly towards the camera, eyes hidden by his trademark novelty kids' sunglasses; Rat Scabies grins impishly as he slurps pie remnants from the Captain's hair, Scabies' own unkempt ginger mop matted with cream; Dave Vanian looks like the victim of a zombie massacre, eyes rolled back in his skull, exposed neck dripping with a viscous red substance which is very likely jam, but which at first glance could almost be mistaken for blood; and Brian James lurks to the right of the picture, as splattered as the rest, but somehow still managing to exude an air of insolent slack-jawed cool, behind a pair of oversized shades. All in all, the image – against a stark black background with the band's name in yellow block capitals – harnesses a bold, unlikely combination of classic rock 'n' roll rebellion, horror movie menace and sheer silliness: seemingly disparate elements which would combine to make the band unique, but also eventually threaten to tear it apart.

The band's contrasting styles were ever more apparent on Erica Echenberg's rear cover live shot (at least, they were once the sleeves were printed with the right image: a supposed printing error meant that initial copies of the

LP bore a photo of contemporary punky pub-rockers, Eddie and the Hot Rods, on the back. In fact, this was a sneaky ploy by Stiff to ensure that these first copies were quickly snapped up as collector's items). Although Rat is largely concealed behind his kit, we still get a clear idea of the striking sight that would have greeted attendees at an early Damned gig. On the right, Brian James is every bit the outlaw guitar hero, with his lank black hair, bare chest and carefully poised Gibson SG, very much in the mould of Johnny Thunders, Wayne Kramer or Keith Richards. In centre stage, Dave Vanian, suited in funereal black, looms vampirically toward the audience, with glossy slicked-back hair and heavily-shadowed eyes to match. The photograph's hand-coloured finish compounds Vanian's ghostly pallor by tinting the other members a healthy pink, while the singer is left in stark monochrome. To the left – turned away from the audience whilst apparently executing a flamboyant high kick – Captain Sensible still makes an impression, mainly due to his choice of a stage attire being a nurse's uniform, helped by his bright shock of orange hair (Ironically, the Captain was somewhat disgruntled that the chosen image didn't show his face, hence the little black-and-white image pasted into the photo on the side of Vanian's monitor speaker).

Released in February 1977, *Damned Damned Damned* climbed to number 36 in the UK chart: a respectable showing for the still-fledgeling Stiff Records, who had yet to sign such future big-hitters as Madness, Elvis Costello and Ian Dury. The release came at a time when tabloid hysteria surrounding punk was running high, sparked by the Sex Pistols' infamously foul-mouthed appearance on the *Today* TV show in December 1976 and further fuelled by the Anarchy tour later that month. This tour featured a dream bill – Sex Pistols, The Clash, The Damned, and former New York Doll, Johnny Thunders, and his new troupe of punk-tinged rock n' rollers, The Heartbreakers – and should have been the perfect chance for UK punk's leading lights to take the new music to all corners of the country, making it a national phenomenon rather than a London-based cult. Sadly, if inevitably, the whole enterprise was dogged by cancellations, bans, protests and controversy, and only seven of around twenty planned dates went ahead. Making matters worse, Malcolm McLaren fired The Damned from the tour before it could even limp to a conclusion, allegedly for agreeing to play a show in Derby after the Pistols had been forbidden to perform. This experience seemed to confirm The Damned's exclusion from punk's 'inner circle' and must have ended 1976 on a sour note for them.

However, with *Damned Damned Damned*, they launched into 1977 in spectacular form, getting one over on their contemporaries, releasing what was not only indisputably the first UK punk LP, but also a startlingly powerful musical statement; one which must have left the Pistols feeling both peeved to be beaten to the punch, and a little intimidated (although I'm sure they would never have admitted any such thing). With The Damned's audience rapidly growing from a small group of local oddballs to a real national following, the momentum seemed unstoppable. Nothing could possibly go wrong ... could it?

'Neat Neat Neat' (Brian James)

The story of British punk on LP begins with one of the meanest riffs the genre has ever produced, played on a bass guitar. In the key of F#, with syncopated slurs up from the F a semitone below, leaping up a minor third to A toward the end of each phrase, it clearly echoes the 1950s rebel twang of Eddie Cochran and Duane Eddy but sped-up and scuzzed-up for the sleazy 1970s. The Captain plays his Hofner violin bass with a fat mid-heavy tone on the cusp of slipping into overdrive, with none of the percussive clank we're used to hearing in many modern bass tones. Notably, rather than playing the riff on the instrument's low E string for the most bassy effect, Sensible chooses to take it up an octave into standard guitar range. It has been suggested that the Captain played bass like he was playing lead guitar, and I can see how one would arrive at that conclusion. But I think it's fairer to say his style combined both bass and rhythm guitar duties, filling up enough sonic space to allow Brian James to take lead breaks without leaving the band sounding empty. The violin bass was the perfect instrument for this, with its warm-but-punchy tone and short-scale length, which made nimble runs and string bends far more manageable than they would be on a full-scale bass (albeit with some intonation niggles and loss of sustain as a trade-off). It may also be worth mentioning that Paul McCartney used the same model in The Beatles' early years when his bold melodic approach redefined the role of bass guitar in pop music. Sensible may not have revered Macca, but perhaps by coincidence, the Captain ended up using the same instrument to surprisingly similar effect.

After we've heard the riff twice, a couple of snare flams set us off and running, with a feral howl from Vanian and some spiky Chuck Berry double-stops from James. The verses cool off slightly, chugging along ominously on that low F#, with an aggressively accented A chord highlighting each line's last word. Vanian's singing here (and on the rest of the LP) immediately marks him out as one of punk's most distinctive vocalists. The rich matinee idol croon heard on many of the group's later records isn't quite there yet, but there's already a hint of a deeper, more dramatic vocal quality than one might expect to hear from a mere punk singer; and while the obligatory rebel sneer is definitely present, it's a little more 'young Brando' and less 'cockney street urchin' than most of Vanian's peers in the UK scene.

The lyrics may not make the most sense, but Vanian snarls them with such authority that it never occurs to us to question them. On closer inspection, verse one introduces our narrator: self-proclaimed 'kinda mystery man'; the object of his interest, a 'baby doll', in a dangerous world where the 'distant man ... can't uphold his distant laws'. With three snare hits punctuating the shout of 'Neatneatneat!', the band powers into the chorus, cranking up the volume and jumping up to A major. Now the lyrics switch focus to the aforementioned 'baby doll', who is clearly in peril and seeking protection, but 'Can't afford no gun at all' and 'Ain't got no name to call'. Verse two elaborates on the anarchic state of affairs alluded to earlier, where there's 'no crime if there ain't no law'. To our 'mystery man', this situation clearly presents an opportunity for some nefarious activity, as he's 'Feelin' fine in her restless time / My mind's on when she falls asleep'. Rather than him wanting to convey any misogyny, I suggest that James' intention was simply to evoke the romanticized Hollywood image of the lawless Wild West and the compelling menace of the horror movie stalker. His words may not stand up to literary scrutiny, but, when sung by Vanian, they do a great job of conveying a sense of nihilistic rebellion and insolent cool.

Released as The Damned's second single, on the same day as its parent LP, 'Neat Neat Neat' has been a fan favourite and a Damned live set staple from the very beginning to the present day. It still stands as one of the greatest songs the genre has produced and is one of the finest album openers I can think of.

'Fan Club' (Brian James)

After the free-wheeling first track has slammed to an abrupt halt, 'Fan Club' takes the pace down several notches, opening with a slithery string-bending minor-key riff from James, setting up the song's smoky mid-tempo groove. The verse anchors itself to a three-chord pattern in B, with James' guitar adding the gnarly dissonance of a flattened 5th (the 'Devil's interval' so beloved of metalheads everywhere!). Over this, Vanian paints a picture of a jaded star observing his fawning audience with a mixture of pity and contempt ('Waiting for an autograph, well you must be mad / Standing in the pissing rain must be a drag'), until in verse three, the pity and contempt are turned inwards, as the star acknowledges himself as 'The freak that's on display': putting on a show for the public while entertaining suicidal thoughts in private, needing a haze of intoxicants to block out the pain. It's a remarkably cynical tale of the bleak consequences of accepting rock 'n' roll's Faustian pact, especially from a band who were only just getting their first glimpse of success. But Vanian puts it across convincingly, in a world-weary half-sung drawl ranging from an angry snarl to a defeated murmur, as our protagonist wonders why he feels sad 'for my fan club', as the tumult of the chorus suddenly gives way to silence. It's a powerful second track, well-placed after 'Neat Neat Neat', showing that The Damned are just as capable of creating atmosphere and tension as they are of dealing in raw power and velocity.

'I Fall' (Brian James)

If 'Fan Club' shows us that – even at this early stage – The Damned understand how to use dynamics, 'I Fall' finds them with their foot firmly back on the gas, with all thought of subtlety out the window. One of several of the LP's songs which began life with James' former group, Bastard, 'I Fall' is a brisk, unrelenting rocker, clocking in at a lean 2:05, with not a second wasted. The verses find James alternating between A and C, blending chugging power chords with sharp, stabbing little lead breaks, while Sensible's propulsive bass riff keeps an underlying A pedal note going throughout. Beneath all this,

Scabies provides some serious Keith Moon-style *sturm und drang*, taking the song from a simmer to a boil, with a wash of ride cymbal and a continuous barrage of cascading tom fills.

The lyrics don't amount to much beyond a fairly generic evocation of frustration and darkness, littered with one or two clunky phrases. But Vanian spits them out with faultless conviction, and with vocal harmonies on the middle eight, a great dumb shout-along chorus (just the title repeated over and over, naturally) and a furious, stinging solo from James, the overall effect is very convincing. Apparently, this was Sensible's preferred choice for a first single, over 'New Rose'. For me, it's not in the same class, but if this is not one of the LP's most remarkable tracks, it only goes to show how high the standard is overall.

'Born To Kill' (Brian James)

The lyrics set the menacing tone. Our protagonist is a bad guy! He commits crimes! He is – as he repeatedly reminds us – born to kill! And that's about it, apart from a couple of references to potential sexual involvement with an unspecified woman, which seem thrown in as an afterthought. It's left to Dave Vanian to make something substantial of this rather thin material, and to his credit, he does a great job, eschewing the aggressive approach the violence-themed lyrics might seem to invite, instead adopting an insouciant mid-Atlantic drawl which is somehow much more effective. The casual, almost bored tone in which he relates his apparent psychosis turns a song that could easily have been little more than a howling cliché into something rather more chilling.

Musically, it's another juggernaut, building on another so-stupid-it's-genius two-chord riff, interspersing nifty 'In the Midnight Hour'-style descending sequences between the verse lines. Rat and the Captain, as ever, provide a mixture of rock-solid foundation and wild pyrotechnics. The track fades out at around the two-and-a-half-minute mark, with James blasting out frantic runs at the top end of the fretboard, as Scabies pounds his kick drum eight-to-the-bar.

'Stab Yor Back' (Rat Scabies)

At a mere 60 seconds in length, Scabies' sole *Damned Damned Damned* songwriting contribution doesn't mess about. It opens with the wind-tunnel whoosh of a huge heavily-phased drum fill and then takes us on a short, fast, bumpy ride. We lurch straight into the chorus, which is simply the title repeated over the power chords, E, B and C#, underpinned by Scabies' eight-to-the-bar bass drum, which continues throughout the track's brief duration. At the time, it was rare to hear this technique from punk drummers, most of whom would tend to emphasise only beats one and three of the bar with the kick drum, providing a snare back-beat on two and four. By hitting the kick on every half-beat, Scabies provides a much more intense, pummelling accompaniment, betraying the influence of double kick drum pioneers such as Keith Moon and Ginger Baker, as well as contemporary heavy rock/metal players, like Motorhead's Phil Taylor.

The verses allow Vanian to bellow a few more threats to the song's unknown target ('Never gonna live till you're twenty-nine!'), while some mock-villainous laughter over the final chorus tells us the lads may not be taking this entirely seriously. It's a somewhat throwaway but very enjoyable track, with a bluntness, brevity and aggression anticipating the early-1980s hardcore movement. Interestingly, 'Stab Yor Back' appears twice on the 'Neat Neat Neat' B-side – in its original form, and as a rearranged instrumental version entitled 'Singalonga Scabies'!

'Feel the Pain' (Brain James)

A spidery, dissonant guitar lick and an atmospheric swell of cymbals set the scene, letting us know we're moving into distinctly different territory, plunging headlong into the darkness so far only hinted at. Like a punk Vincent Price, Dave Vanian – drenched in spooky echo and clearly in his element – moans, whispers and coos his way through verses laden with creepy, enigmatic and sadomasochistic imagery, relishing the serpentine sibilance of lines like 'Your starched white lips, intravenous she drips'. The band gathers momentum, falling into step on a C minor chord, as Vanian lets his developing baritone croon loose on the chorus, commanding us to 'Feel the pain, it leaves no stain', before we're back to the verse's eerie hush. It's a remarkably restrained performance from a band not exactly renowned for their subtlety, with everyone holding back, allowing Vanian's ghoulish persona free reign.

While most of the LP is clearly sonically indebted to proto-punk garage rockers, The Stooges, MC5 and New York Dolls, there's something quite different going on here. There are clear echoes of the darker, more downbeat moments of The Doors and The Velvet Underground, Alice Cooper's less arty 'shock rock', and the over the top Gothic melodrama of Hammer horror movies. In short, this song effectively invents the goth rock movement in a single stroke. The track serves as a diversion from the up-tempo rock that dominates the LP elsewhere. But in years to come, Vanian, in particular, would continue to develop this aspect, until, by the mid-1980s, it would come to define the band, for better or for worse.

'New Rose' (Brian James)

Just in case 'Feel the Pain's more downbeat approach lulled anyone into a false sense of security, The Damned opted to commence side two with the very first example of British punk rock on record and an absolutely storming high-octane classic to boot. The 'New Rose' single pipped Sex Pistols' 'Anarchy In The UK' at the post by some five weeks, and in doing so, left an indelible mark on the genre, establishing a sound at once harnessing rock 'n' roll's primitive power and energy, and setting new standards of attitude, velocity and aggression. Indeed, for all Johnny Rotten's stunningly obnoxious lyrics, after hearing 'New Rose', some may have found the Pistols' debut a little sedate in comparison.

The song begins with Vanian's spoken line, 'Is she really going out with him?': a tongue-in-cheek reference to The Shangri-Las' 'Leader Of The Pack' (1964), which tells the tragic tale of doomed love for a delinquent from the wrong side of the tracks. Similarly, 'New Rose' is a depiction of new love/lust, this time told from the delinquent's point of view. Scabies sets the pace with a thudding tribal tom-tom rhythm, soon joined by James' raw, overdriven four-chord riff, wrenching a venomous tone from his Gibson SG and 100-watt Hi-Watt stack (the same guitar/amp combination Pete Townshend used during The Who's early-1970s peak). After a yell from Vanian, Sensible's bass crashes in as the band hits full-throttle, not letting up. The remainder of the song's two minutes and 43 seconds absolutely tears by in a blur of sleazy New York Dolls-ish riffage, an unrelenting barrage of clattering percussion, and an excitable, half-sung/half-yelled vocal. As John Savage says in his essential chronicle of the birth of UK punk, *England's Dreaming*:

> 'New Rose' is a pure rush of enthusiasm, of people finding their power ... The storyline - of the excitement of a new love affair – parallels The Damned's exultation in making noise.

Over the years, several artists have covered the song, ranging from cult-ish indie rockers, Gumball, to stadium-filling behemoths Guns N' Roses. The song also appears on numerous live albums by later Damned line-ups, but nothing matches the original recording. It's the distilled essence of early UK punk rock, and more than forty years later, it's still a thrilling listen.

'Fish' (Brian James – Thanx Tony (Tony James))
Following 'New Rose' was always going to be tough, so the band don't really try, opting instead for this brief, silly diversion. A co-writing credit to Tony James (later of Generation X and Sigue Sigue Sputnik) seems to date the song's origin to Brian and Rat's stint in London SS, and indeed there's a bit of a pre-punk pub rock feel to the Chuck Berry rhythm guitar chug and Scabies' four-on-the-floor stomp. Brian James, it must be admitted, was prone to settling for a throwaway lyric, but it's rescued by the band's performance. They attack the song with boundless energy, conviction and enthusiasm, with James, in particular, turning in a jaw-dropping solo. The whole thing crashes to an abrupt conclusion well inside the two-minute mark.

'See Her Tonite' (Brian James)
Just when proceedings were in danger of flagging slightly, things really kick up a gear. A brisk yell of 'One, two, three, go!', and the band rockets out of the starting blocks in unison, at an even more frantic pace than the preceding tracks. The majority of early punk records adhere more or less to the rhythmic template The Ramones laid down (The de facto first proper punk band), keeping to a swift 4/4 time with a solid backbeat and eighth notes on the hi-

hat or ride cymbals. The majority of *Damned Damned Damned* tracks take
this approach, albeit with Scabies' interesting variations thrown in (He was
never a drummer who cared much for rules). However, 'See Her Tonite' takes
a different tack, with a 2/4 rhythm rattling the song along at a breakneck clip.
As the turn of the decade approached and newer, more 'hardcore' punk bands
placed a greater emphasis on speed and aggression, this kind of pared-down
2/4 rhythm would come to dominate the genre. Although The Damned would
frequently utilise a hard and fast 2/4 attack on subsequent albums, Rat would
always imbue the rhythm with considerably more swing and flair than many
of the heads-down thrashers he had undoubtedly helped to inspire. At this
velocity, there's a sense that everything could fall apart at any moment. But
the band pull it off admirably, with Scabies filling every available space with
nimble fills and cymbal accents, and James pounding out a steady rhythm in
the left channel, overdubbing searing leads and dramatic ringing chord work
on the right.

The lyric – which mirrors all of this excitement – finds our narrator enthusing
over a young woman in whom he has found a kindred spirit/like-minded
weirdo ('She's so cool! See her tonight!'). It's refreshing to hear a song where
the narrator loves a girl for her intelligence and what she has to say.

The chorus is where 'See Her Tonite' really goes from being solid album
filler to something special. At the first chorus, we find Vanian crooning over
a chord sequence of E minor/G/C/B, bolstered by some nifty harmonies. So
far, so good, but nothing outstanding. The second time, the first two chorus
lines are a direct repeat. However, just as we are being lulled into familiarity,
we're suddenly plunged into a different key for the next two lines, in a bold,
yearning sequence of F# minor/A/E/G. It's hard to explain the musical effect
accurately, suffice it to say that this shift in harmony – combined with the
falsetto backing vocal accompanying it – is one of those rare, pulse-quickening
'lightning in a bottle' moments that can lift a pop song to another plane
in an instant. Moreover, in a genre that initially relied heavily on amped-
up reworkings of rock 'n' roll's basic building blocks, this is a rare flash of
compositional sophistication, hinting at the direction the band would take a
few years later with the likes of 'Melody Lee' from *Machine Gun Etiquette*. After
a third soaring chorus, the song climaxes with stabbing chord punctuations
and Scabies hammering out a spectacular run of light-speed triplet fills before
finally crashing to a conclusion – the band members whooping with exultation,
as well they might. The song is a definite highlight, and every bit the equal of
the more widely-known singles.

'1 of the 2' (Brian James)
A bleak depiction of degradation and debasement, '1 of the 2' takes off at a
strident mid-tempo stomp, a solo squall of abrasive lead guitar punctuating
each first verse line (joined by Scabies' booming tom rolls on subsequent
verses). Vanian imbues the vocal with a suitable air of contempt, his sneering

'That's the way down ... that's sedation ... one of the two!' given extra emphasis through cavernous echo (one of few noticeable production tricks Lowe allows on the album). It's a solid song and a cracking performance. If anything, with a repeat of the first verse and a third chorus, , not really adding anything other than length, it slightly outstays its welcome. However, the outro breaks the predictability nicely, building to a tense crescendo over the chords of C and B before snapping to an abrupt halt. Certainly not a bad track then, but not the album's most essential song either, doomed to fall slightly flat after the breathtaking rush of 'See Her Tonite'.

'So Messed Up' (Brian James)
Another song which, in the grand Ramones tradition, begins with a yelled count-in – in this case, 'One, two, three, oh she's so ... ' – before launching into a diatribe so spectacularly idiotic that it makes the aforementioned 'brothers' from Queens sound like fey intellectuals by comparison. It's less a fully-formed song than a few lines of schoolboy doggerel; crude even by early punk rock standards, and it lacks the edgy wit and ear for a catchy phrase that James brings to a lyric when he puts his mind to it. Instead, here we have Vanian gamely intoning such lyrical gems as 'She's a sad case of hit and run / I think that I would rather fuck her mum'.

Similarly, the musical accompaniment seems to lack the spark that is so apparent throughout the rest of the LP; the bands chugs along steadily enough for a minute or so, dropping to a half-time feel and then building to a crescendo as the title repeats over and over, after which everything clatters to a messy standstill ... and then starts again, for another half-minute of more of the same. It's certainly not all negative – the band still sounds terrific, and their attitude and enthusiasm are ever-infectious. But compared to the other material we've heard, this really is a bit sub-par, which is probably why it was buried toward the end of side two.

'I Feel Alright' (Dave Alexander, Ron Asheton, Scott Asheton, Iggy Pop)
It's not unreasonable to suggest that every single band from punk's first wave owed some kind of debt to The Stooges. From the most cerebral experimentalists to the most basic three-chord thrashers, all bore some imprint of Iggy and the gangs' nihilistic, wilfully primitive, artifice-and-pretension-stripped take on rock. However, it's also fair to say that of all of the UK's first wave; none was closer in sound to the scuzzy, spiteful garage rock of Detroit's finest than the original Brian James-led incarnation of The Damned. Therefore, it's quite fitting that they should acknowledge this clear influence by closing their debut platter with a cover of the Stooges classic, '1970'. To keep things sounding contemporary and to avoid referencing the worryingly-hippy-ish era of seven years earlier, the band use the repeated chorus refrain 'I feel alright' as a new title; Vanian managing to mangle the lyric's mention of the titular year

into 'Nineteen seventy-seven, baby, rolling in sight', which does little for the song's scansion, but presumably adds some punk credibility.

While The Damned have some obvious sonic traits in common with The Stooges – particularly James' raw, slashing guitar style, with its Ron Asheton-like melding of stinging lead lines and a burst of furious avant-garde noise – listening to the two song versions side by side reveals some notable differences, which show us that The Damned were not content to simply ape their influences. In a straight comparison, poor Dave Vanian is always going to have the roughest deal, as his still-developing baritone of the era was no match for Iggy's incomparable crazed yowl: part Jim Morrison moan, part Howlin' Wolf blues holler, but with an air of menace and depravity which is entirely his own. Nevertheless, Vanian does a perfectly acceptable job, delivering the song with a distinctive deadpan sneer, and the fact that he doesn't attempt to mimic Pop's inimitably-unhinged style is absolutely to Vanian's credit; plenty of others have tried, and the results are rarely convincing and often embarrassing.

After a couple of declamatory chords and some primaeval whooping, James hammers out the bludgeoning two-chord riff, setting a slightly faster tempo than the original, hitting his low E string beneath the two chords, creating a texture somewhat darker and sludgier than Asheton's. Rat joins in with the riff, initially emphasising the backbeat with snare flams, before ushering in the full band with one of his trademark round-the-kit fills. Significantly, rather than copying Scott Asheton's distinctive ostinato pattern – which repeats with little variation save for a few accents throughout the Stooges' recording – Scabies opts for a straight-ahead 2/4 kick-snare rhythm. This approach loses the tribal-sounding and almost hypnotic effect of the original record but gives the song a great deal more forward motion. Indeed, without wishing to dwell too much on the respective musicians' pharmaceutical indulgences, The Stooges' '1970' is very much a stoner record, with its trance-like repetition, wah-wah guitar freak-outs and saxophone noodling. In comparison, The Damned's 'I Feel Alright' is a definite product of amphetamine consumption, with its accelerated tempo and pared-down driving rhythmic attack, charging headlong towards the finish line.

The Stooges recording of '1970' is over five minutes long, and with The Damned's version clocking in at nearly four and a half (the LP's longest track by some margin), one might assume they followed the original's structure fairly closely. However, while The Stooges stretch out – interspersing the verses and choruses with loose, jammed-out instrumental passages, culminating in an extended out-chorus serving as a launch pad for some wild tenor sax improvisation from Steve Mackay – The Damned rocket through the three verses and choruses and an especially-venomous guitar solo, in record time. Then, at around the three-minute mark, the track dissolves into utter chaos, the LP concluding with 90 seconds of pure anarchic noise. This serves not only to act as a sort of miniature version of The Stooges' 'L.A. Blues' – the free-jazz/noise experiment that closed the *Fun House* album from which '1970' was taken – but also to mimic the auto-destructive cacophony which often concluded The Damned's stage show, further enhancing the 'live' illusion created through Nick Lowe's minimal production. Overall, it's a strong finish to an incendiary debut, honouring the architects of punk while making a strong case for The Damned as its leading practitioners.

Music for Pleasure (1977)

Personnel:
Lu Edmonds: guitar
Brian James: guitar
Captain Sensible: bass Guitar and vocals
Rat Scabies: drums
Dave Vanian: vocals
Additional Personnel:
Lol Coxhill: saxophone on 'You Know'
Recorded at Britannia Row Studios, London
Record label: Stiff Records
Released: 18 November 1977
Producer: Nick Mason
Highest UK chart position: did not chart
Length: 33:50
Current edition: 2015 Sanctuary Records reissue

Following the debut album's release, the first half of 1977 was quite a whirlwind for the band. First, they toured the UK supporting T. Rex – Marc Bolan being a rare member of pop's older guard who was excited and energised, rather than horrified, by punk – and converted a fair few surprisingly receptive glam fans along the way. They followed this by beating their UK punk scene peers to the punch once again, becoming the first British punk band to tour the US. Punk was born in the States, with New York's CBGB club as ground zero, and small regional scenes had tentatively begun to germinate in other areas. The Dead Boys had recently risen from the ashes of Cleveland proto-punk mavericks, Rocket From The Tombs. While on the west coast, The Germs were taking the first faltering steps of a brief, spectacularly self-destructive run, which would lay the groundwork for the L.A. hardcore scene. However, beyond these small scenes – and the writings of a few niche critics – the genre was largely unknown and had certainly made no noticeable impact on a mainstream very much in the twin thrall of disco and the radio-friendly 'adult-oriented rock' being churned out by a generation of ex-hippies who had traded 1960s radicalism for cynical commercialism. Against this backdrop, The Damned cut a bold, pioneering path across America, meeting with open hostility in some areas but undoubtedly inspiring a lot of the disaffected young people who came to see them.

Certainly, many of the punk acts who emerged throughout the US in 1977 and 1978 – The Misfits from New Jersey, TSOL from Long Beach and The Avengers from San Francisco etc. – betrayed the clear influence of The Damned's aggressive, high-energy style. The Misfits in particular – who would go on to be hugely influential on the 1980s hardcore and heavy metal scenes – took The Damned's musical template and Dave Vanian's ghoulish image as their own, exaggerating them to cartoonish effect.

Returning from the States, The Damned embarked on another lengthy UK jaunt, this time headlining, with fellow London scenesters, The Adverts, in tow. The Damned had taken their music to the masses, succeeding in expanding their audience considerably. However, by this stage, they were no longer the only British punk band with an LP – The Clash, The Stranglers, The Jam and The Vibrators all released their debut long-players by June 1977 – and the pressure was on to come up with something new. As principal songwriter, Brian James especially felt this pressure; the songs on *Damned Damned Damned* had come together over a number of years, with several having their basis in ideas he'd worked on in his previous groups, Bastard and London SS. Now, in a matter of a few short months, he was expected to come up with something fresh which would consolidate the first record's success, plus move the band's sound forward. His first step towards achieving this demanding goal was to expand the band's line-up. Adding second guitarist Robert 'Lu' Edmonds turned The Damned into a five-piece, like James' beloved MC5: a move which left his bandmates nonplussed to say the least. Captain Sensible, speaking to John Robb for his book, *Punk Rock: An Oral History* later said:

> I don't think it worked in the slightest! No disrespect to Lu, who was a lovely bloke, but The Damned only needed one guitar ... The two-guitar thing can work, but Lu and Brian were not like the MC5 blokes.

Following the new-look Damned's debut performance at the second Mont de Marsan punk festival (in August), they were booked into a studio to record the hastily-assembled new material, with unlikely 'name' producer, Nick Mason, drummer of Pink Floyd: a band whose thoughtful, experimental and occasionally pretentious 1970s output had made them the target of much mockery and vitriol from the first generation UK punks (Johnny Rotten was often seen wearing an 'I Hate Pink Floyd' t-shirt). The story surrounding the situation is somewhat confused. Sensible has always maintained that they were hoping to work with Syd Barrett: the visionary behind Floyd's psychedelic debut, *The Piper at the Gates of Dawn* (1967). However, following the deterioration of Barrett's mental health, he'd been living a reclusive life in Cambridge for years, so he was never likely to come out of retirement to produce a bunch of upstart punks. The truth is that the plan was always for Mason to produce the LP at Floyd's own Britannia Row Studios, but Syd Barrett made for a more punk-credible story to tell the press. Some commentators (Brian James included) have blamed *Music for Pleasure*'s relative failure on Mason's production, but this is rather unfair. Certainly, he didn't understand The Damned's music or way of working, as well as Nick Lowe did; Pink Floyd's painstakingly methodical recording process couldn't be further from the fast-'n'-cheap approach taken by Lowe, so the two parties definitely arrived in the studio with differing expectations. The resulting product doesn't sound bad by any means; it just comes across as a little subdued and slightly too clean compared with the fearsome blast that is *Damned Damned Damned*. The real problems at the heart of *Music for Pleasure* were some rather half-baked material and a growing sense of disillusionment within the band, neither of which could be blamed on Mason. In retrospect, taken on its own merits, the record definitely contains a handful of great tracks, and even the weaker material is largely good, solid 1977 punk. Unfortunately, the first LP set a very high bar, and with debut platters by The Clash and The Stranglers upping the ante considerably, this rushed and somewhat fraught effort was always destined to be slightly disappointing in comparison – for the band and listeners alike.

Packaged in an elaborate Barney Bubbles-designed gatefold sleeve – featuring a gaudy Kandinsky-inspired abstraction on the front, and 3D-treated photographs of the band inside – *Music for Pleasure* was released on 18 November 1977 received largely negative reviews, failed to chart, and promptly sank without a trace. After starting the year with such aplomb, everything started falling apart for The Damned: Scabies left shortly after recording the LP, and Stiff dropped the band soon thereafter. They struggled on for a short while – first with drummer, Dave Berk, from Johnny Moped, and then Jon Moss, later of Culture Club fame – but enthusiasm was waning, and in early 1978, Brian James announced that he also was leaving the band, effectively ending The Damned's first incarnation.

'Problem Child' (Rat Scabies, Brian James)

For all that we know of the challenging circumstances surrounding this album's creation, it actually begins on a triumphant note. 'Problem Child' is a simple but effective rocker, dripping with attitude and tongue-in-cheek humour, which is absolutely up to the high standard set by the group's debut. Rather than launching straight into a full-bore assault, tension builds gradually through the verse, the guitars steadily chugging 8th notes on a muted A chord, as Rat softly taps his snare, gently swelling in volume, but audibly holding back, until there's a sudden dead stop. Then, a solid thwack of tom-toms brings us into a great, stomping chorus in E, releasing all the verse's pent-up aggression before simmering back down with Scabies' Keith Moon-like flourishes, ready to restart the build-up.

Over all of this, Dave Vanian assumes the role of the titular juvenile delinquent, in what is effectively an update of Larry Williams' R&B classic, 'Bad Boy' (1959), for the punk generation. Each verse details aspects of his 'problematic' behaviour, ranging from fairly standard teen disobedience ('I wanna come home at 3 AM') to the downright alarming ('I gave a dose to my sister'), ending with a spoken punchline reminiscent of Eddie Cochran's rather more innocent ode to youthful transgression: 'Summertime Blues'. ('Now you can't use the car 'cause you didn't work a lick' etc.). As we enter the chorus, the narrative voice shifts, signified musically through the shift from Vanian's solo voice to a group vocal, complete with rough and ready harmonies acting as a sort of Greek chorus, commenting on the problem child's behaviour, warning him that 'When you get home, your daddy's gonna tan your hide!'

Structurally, it's straightforward, with a one-chord verse, a three-chord chorus, and no middle-eights or instrumentals to complicate matters. However, the band really lift the song through a dynamic ensemble performance worthy of The Who's classic run of mid-1960s singles. Scabies is particularly impressive, moving from passages of remarkably restrained accompaniment, to his trademark flurries of flashy aggression, with a great sense of musicality. Vanian provides a spirited vocal, injecting just the right level of arch attitude to the spoken interjections capping each verse, and Sensible's bass powers the track along, throwing in a raunchy flat-7th, giving the chorus an extra hint of rock 'n' roll flair. In fact, it's only the new James and Edmonds guitar partnership who don't especially distinguish themselves here, filling out the sound adequately and matching the band's dynamics, but with no hint of the MC5-like interplay, James had hoped for. Instead – both here and at other points throughout the LP – the presence of another player seems to slightly constrain James. On *Damned Damned Damned*, he used his two tracks to create a simulated partnership: at times, playing in tight unison for a focused attack; at others, expanding the sound with complementary lines, providing a backing to his own lead pyrotechnics. On *Music for Pleasure*, the two guitars rarely interact so effectively; there's nothing wrong with either musician's playing, but the chemistry – all-important to a great pairing – is sadly lacking.

Nevertheless, 'Problem Child' remains a powerful album opener. Released as the album's first single (The 'Stretcher Case Baby' single was a different recording to the LP version), it failed to chart, but deserved much better. It was one of the few songs from the album to make its way into the band's post-1977 live sets and is now rightfully accepted as a minor Damned classic.

'Don't Cry Wolf' (Brian James)

'Don't Cry Wolf' ratchets up the momentum even further. It opens with a solo guitar, accompanied only by Rat, keeping time on the hi-hat. The riff is basic in content, with power chords of B flat and C, returning to a root of G. However, rather than these chords being an unbroken barrage of 8th notes *ala* Johnny Ramone, James adds rests between the chords, using space to create syncopation and generate rhythmic interest. The resulting pattern is reminiscent of AC/DC: the antipodean hard-rockers who were growing greatly in popularity at the time and whose stripped-down approach made them palatable to punks who might normally shun such fare. After a couple of repetitions, Scabies brings the rhythm in, throwing in some unexpectedly funky offbeat snare ghost notes alongside his usual explosive fills. The introduction of the bass and second guitar with a whole-tone leap to the key of A really kicks the track into gear. Now the full band launches into a second riff, even harder-rocking and more redolent of AC/DC than the first, although Rat's frenetic percussion keeps it from settling into the kind of steady, solid groove the Young brothers favoured.

Over a rising ringing-chord sequence and a stomping drum rhythm, Vanian delivers the lyric's incitement to rebellion: 'You don't have to listen to what your parents say / They don't understand us, their laws we don't obey.' This anti-conformity schtick is fairly bog-standard punk subject matter, expressed in terms that must have sounded a little generic even back in 1977. Nevertheless, the band's vigorous performance and Vanian's authoritative delivery somehow combine to give these cliches the weight of punk rock commandments, culminating in a chant of 'Don't be a fool, don't cry wolf', delivered over the crunching main riff. A brief middle eight leads us to an intro reprise, bolstered by some tasty lead guitar stabs. A mass of overdubbed handclaps keeping the beat, nod to a similar section in the New York Dolls' 'Jet Boy' (1973), a formative Damned influence. After a verse one repeat, we launch into a final double-length chorus, with the right-channel guitar soaring up an octave, heightening the sense of urgency, which is increased even further by another whole-tone key change – up to B – for the closing eight bars.

Released as a single on 11 December 1977, 'Don't Cry Wolf' failed to capture the fickle record-buying public's attention but became a popular part of the band's 1979 reunion tour live sets, and stands up today as a great slice of skilfully arranged, powerfully played, rock 'n' roll.

'One Way Love' (Brian James)

In this chapter's introduction, I suggested that *Music for Pleasure* could be considered something of a disappointment. But here we are, three tracks in, with no sign of a let-up in quality so far. Could I have been too hasty in my judgement? Well, we'll see.

After a barnstorming opening brace of songs, 'One Way Love' ramps the tempo up even further, taking off at an amazingly blistering pace. The James/Edmonds guitar partnership (which fails to inspire for much of the LP) really clicks into place here, with Brian's fierce lead fills offsetting Lu's hard-edged riffing, recapturing some of that fire so evident throughout *Damned Damned Damned*. An interesting addition is a third guitar track, on which James adds a glassy, reverb-drenched slide guitar – common in blues and country recordings but rarely heard in punk circles – lending the track a surprisingly ethereal edge. A relatively long song by Damned standards in 1977, the track appears to be about to halt around the 3:15 mark, only to lurch into an entirely new out-chorus section for the final 30 seconds before coming to rest on a ringing A minor chord.

If 'One Way Love' has a weak point, it's the lyrics. As we've previously noted, Brian James is occasionally prone to falling back on overused tropes, so here we have the standard 'warning a friend about a girl who is bad news' scenario, which is rather hackneyed: 'She's the fastest girl in town / She ain't worried who's been shooting her / Bad boy shooters from around.' Obviously, Dave Vanian manages to make even James' clunkiest lines sound credible, but here and elsewhere on the LP, there is a sense that the pressure of having to come up with a lot of material in a short space of time has led the band to settle for a somewhat sub-par lyric, which is a pity, given that the music is so strong.

'Politics' (Brian James)

Politics and punk have had a long, volatile relationship. Every conceivable political creed has had a band – or sometimes even an entire subgenre – represent it: from the anarcho-punk movement (spearheaded by Crass), which provided a focal point for anarchism in the early-to-mid 1980s; to the vile 'Blood & Honour' organisation (led by Skrewdriver) which had a similarly galvanising effect on the neo-Nazi skinhead movement; and everything in-between. Back in 1977, these extremes had yet to emerge, but the music was already playing with political ideas: from the Ramones' tongue-in-cheek right-wing authoritarianism to the Sex Pistols' call for 'Anarchy in the UK'; and following the release of The Clash's self-titled debut, more and more bands were leaning towards Strummer and Jones' gritty social realism and street-level political rhetoric. It is this trend that seems to have prompted James to pen the imaginatively titled, 'Politics', in which he protests that 'I don't need no politics to make me dance' and 'Give me fun, not anarchy'. I suppose it's understandable that he wanted to avoid following his contemporaries into a cul-de-sac of shallow, tokenistic political songwriting, but as a lyric, this feels rather weak and unnecessary; The Damned had already established their own niche, celebrating rebellion and nihilism with an inimitably-cartoonish blend of darkness and humour, and had no need to justify themselves, or measure themselves against anyone else in the scene. Ironically, the band's post-James incarnation soon developed a knack for working sociopolitical commentary into songs without compromising the original spirit of chaotic fun, one iota.

In musical terms, 'Politics' is brimming with energy – founded on an absolutely belting guitar riff – and has an unusual and engaging verse melody but is let down by a damp squib of a chorus that doesn't really go anywhere. Also, Scabies – truly one of punk's greatest drummers – has some timing issues in the verses (unusual for him), somehow losing half a beat in-between his busy fills, creating the impression that the song is tripping over its own feet. Ultimately, it feels like 'Politics' could have used a little more work and time in the practice room before being committed to vinyl.

'Stretcher Case' (Rat Scabies / Brian James)

While most of *Music for Pleasure* was written in a short space of time and specifically for the record, 'Stretcher Case' originated a little earlier. The four-piece Damned recorded a version in May 1977 and released it on 3 July as a limited edition fan club single to mark the band's first anniversary. It was produced by Shel Talmy: the legendary American maverick behind such pivotal pop history moments as The Who's 'My Generation' (1965), The Kinks' 'You Really Got Me' (1964), and scores of others. While not in the same league as these milestones, the original version – fully titled 'Stretcher Case Baby', backed with another forthright rocker, titled 'Sick Of Being Sick' – is 2:16 of fierce, stripped-down punk, very much continuing the no-frills, high-energy approach of the debut album.

In its album form, 'Stretcher Case' is abbreviated in both title and length: rearranged to a lean 1:52 running time and shorn of the false ending – perhaps because they'd already employed a similar trick on 'One Way Love'.

Like the original, 'Stretcher Case' begins with Rat playing a rumbling tom roll straight out of The Surfaris' 'Wipe Out', soon joined by James and Edmonds' guitars thrashing out a C# chord. The twin guitar attack adds little to this new version, although Lu (in the left channel) adds a minor 3rd to James' power chord (the root and 5th), giving the track a slightly darker, explicitly minor-key tonality. The Talmy recording – perhaps deliberately recreating the mono of his 1960s classics – mixes everything centrally, creating a compressed wall of sound, whereas Mason makes full use of the stereo spectrum. A comparison of the two recordings reveals that, although Talmy's more raw approach may capture the band's in-your-face aggression more immediately, Mason's cleaner, more spacious production allows us to appreciate finer details, with Scabies' ever-frantic fills cascading from left to right, and some rare Brian James solo vocal moments highlighted to the right side (He can be heard delivering the interjection 'problem!' between chorus phrases, and the spoken final line of each verse). Vanian and James' contrasting vocal interplay – Vanian's commanding baritone and James' louche drawl – is very effective here, and one wonders why they didn't repeat the trick elsewhere.

The track positively charges along, tense, churning verses in C# minor exploding into a pounding chorus in E with a great call and response vocal hook. As is often the case with early Damned songs, only the lyrics slightly let the side down. Whilst the words drip with unmistakable malice, which is vividly mirrored in the music, the actual target remains nebulous: the first verse seems to reject an unwanted romantic advance, while the third is an outright threat of violence ('Sucker wanna pay, so what do you say?') I'm not quite sure what's meant to be happening in verse two; suffice it to say that it involves a 'thirty-year-old whore' and an autopsy! Frankly, it's a little incoherent, and the lack of a regular syllable pattern or rhyme scheme means Vanian has to stretch and mangle the lyric considerably to make it fit the available space. Still, 'Stretcher Case' absolutely oozes attitude and aggression, and in that respect, captures The Damned at their best.

'Idiot Box' (Captain Sensible / Rat Scabies)
Having had a hand in writing two of the album's clear stand-out tracks, Rat's third songwriting contribution here (and the Captain's first on any Damned record) is a bit of an oddity. 'Idiot Box', of course, is a synonym for Television: in this case, not the living room appliance, but the artsy New York proto-punks who – along with the Ramones, Blondie and Talking Heads – emerged from the primordial swamp of the CBGB scene. The Damned's spring US tour in

1977 had scheduled a show with Television at L.A.'s Whisky au Go Go. But by the time they reached the west coast, it emerged that Television frontman Tom Verlaine had requested The Damned be removed from the bill. Perhaps Patti Smith – who had clashed with The Damned during their earlier CBGB residency – had warned Verlaine off, or maybe word of their show-stealing and often highly irresponsible antics on the tour, had reached him by other channels. Either way, The Damned were off the gig, and having previously been Television fans, they were bitterly disappointed.

'Idiot Box' then, is a revenge of sorts, taking lyrical swipes at Television members whilst parodying their musical style, eschewing The Damned's usual furious power chord adrenalin, for a measured, brooding sound with some jazz chords and a decent stab at some Verlaine-esque modal lead guitar. There are some nice touches, though: the main riff, in particular, uses deceptively simple ingredients to surprisingly sophisticated effect; the lead guitar line – a simple double-stop on the high E and B strings, moving from the fifth to seventh fret, rounded off with a bluesy G-string bend – sounds like a fairly standard rock 'n' roll device in the key of A. However, when the bass enters, the key is established as D, the guitar line now an enigmatic ringing suspended-9th over the D bass root. An extended instrumental section in the second half – based around the distinctly un-Damned-like chords of Em/Sus4 and F#m/Sus4 – also does a decent job of parodying Television's studied cerebral style.

However, the song itself almost seems like an afterthought to these parodic touches, with little in the way of melody, and the 4:49 running time seems bloated for such a slight effort. Additionally, Scabies – a magnificent drummer when being himself – in attempting to parody Billy Ficca's jazzy frills and polyrhythmic inflexions, ends up simply sounding uncharacteristically clumsy and sloppy. Similarly, though the lyrics contain the occasional half-decent put-down ('Tom Verlaine, you may be art / But you sure ain't rock 'n' roll'), they're pretty toothless on the whole ('Old Fred Smith works for the box / Oh what a haggard face'). For a band who were more than capable of being shocking and outrageous, 'Idiot Box' feels like a rather feeble jibe, and one suspects that – had the band had more time to work on new material – this song would not have made the cut.

'You Take My Money' (Brian James)

Side two kicks off with this swaggering, mid-tempo slice of thuggery; an account of a parasitic relationship, with dark hints of violence and drug addiction, anchored to a bludgeoning, repetitive two-chord riff of stone-age simplicity. In fact, the whole song is built on repetition, with every lyric line beginning with the phrase 'You take my money ... ', the same line being repeated on its own as the chorus. Despite the short 2:04 running time, this constant re-use of the phrase over the two-chord pattern (G to E for the chorus and B flat to G for the verse) wears thin rather quickly, especially when delivered at what is, for The Damned, a fairly pedestrian pace.

But they do their best to inject life into the proceedings: Vanian gives it loads of attitude, delivering his asides of 'Honey' with a vitriolic sneer, and Scabies slipping sixteenth hi-hat notes over the four-on-the-floor kick drum (a pattern most often heard on disco records, though, as played by Rat, with not a hint of Studio 54 about it) really lifts the verses. However, there's not a great deal for them to work with, and after a single-note/single-chord middle eight in D briefly breaks the monotony, the song is already played out with nowhere left to go. An unnecessary verse one repeat fills the remaining half-minute before the track plods to an unremarkable conclusion, displaying a lack of inspiration that all of the band's considerable chutzpah can't quite camouflage.

'Alone' (Brian James)

After that, the album desperately needs a shot in the arm, and thankfully, this track delivers. One of two particularly Stooges-influenced songs on the album – and arguably the most successful – 'Alone' was actually one of The Damned's earliest original songs, featuring in their first-ever live set on 6 July 1976. It made several more appearances before being retired, only to be dusted off and revamped a year later, when the demand for new material became pressing.

The song is built on an Asheton-esque circular guitar and drum pattern: a bluesy riff in E, over a clamorous drum ostinato, creating an insistent, tribal throb, which would have sounded very much at home on The Stooges' *Funhouse* album. Rat and Brian are on fire throughout, with James (relatively subdued for much of the LP) wringing some fearsome lead breaks from his SG, blending accomplished shredding solos with sheets of jagged noise, and Scabies powering everything along with seemingly inexhaustible energy and invention. Rising to the occasion, Vanian drops his usual slightly deadpan approach, really letting rip, snarling, ranting and frothing at the mouth in a manner recalling not just Iggy Pop, but some of Alice Cooper's more histrionic excesses. As I suggested while discussing 'I Feel Alright', it's a brave and foolhardy British punk singer who attempts to 'Do an Iggy' – but all credit to Vanian: this is a thoroughly convincing and riveting performance.

Dave Vanian excels at selling The Damned's darker, more menacing material, with a heightened 'film noir villain' archness providing enough edge to create a sense of danger, balanced by theatricality introducing a tongue-in-cheek sense of fun. However, James' lyrics here – cloaked in some clunky attempts at poetic imagery – seem to play with the taboo of sexual violence in a way that is neither tongue-in-cheek nor fun, marring what is otherwise one of the album's stand-out tracks.

'Your Eyes' (Dave Vanian / Brian James)

'Your Eyes' represents Dave Vanian's first songwriting on a Damned record. But unfortunately, there's barely a hint of the dramatic flair or eerie atmospherics that would become his calling card in years to come. Instead, we find our hero in an uncharacteristically sappy, heartbroken mood, pining for the girl who got away and drinking to forget: 'You won't have to look far / I'll be in the nearest bar / I feel so very cold / And I'm feeling so very old.' It's all rather 'moon in June', and the accompanying music is similarly pedestrian: a mid-tempo slouch centred around a not-especially-memorable riff oscillating lazily between A and B minor without ever really going anywhere. Scabies and Sensible do their best to provide some rhythm section interest, throwing in nimble fills here and there, but there really aren't many hooks to keep the listener engaged, and the two minutes and fifty seconds pass very slowly. Vanian and James could write this kind of thing in their sleep, and listening to the record, you could almost believe they did.

'Creep (You Can't Fool Me)' (Brian James)
Happily, things liven up considerably with this slight-but-sprightly broadside against bullies and posers. The 'creep' of the title loves to play the tough guy, 'acting James Dean', but is a coward at heart ('If I look in your eyes, you just run and hide'), with our narrator finally telling him to 'Go and beat up your cat / I bet you're good at that'. Coming from James – whose lyrics can be quite barbed – this is fairly harmless stuff. But given a spirited delivery at a rattling pace, it makes for a diverting two minutes and feels like a breath of fresh air after the lifeless 'Your Eyes'.

Musically, there's nothing approaching a melody, but a busy arrangement that refuses to settle into one key for any length of time, creates interest. Opening on a choppy stop/start riff in D – with Edmunds hammering out the chords and James adding some Chuck Berry double-stops in a higher octave – we progress to a verse which starts in B, moving up to C# halfway through, before landing in A for the chorus, after which the whole pattern starts again.

As I say, there's nothing particularly substantial about this track, but it is a lively, enjoyable little rocker. Still, you can't quite escape the feeling that after a thunderously promising start, the latter half of *Music for Pleasure* is rather running out of steam.

'You Know' (Brian James)
The closing track is the album's most challenging by far. As with 'Alone', 'You Know' draws explicit influence from The Stooges' *Funhouse* LP. However, while the former song shoehorns its Asheton-isms into a relatively conventional and compact three-minute structure, 'You Know' goes all out with bludgeoning intensity and trance-like repetition. Almost the whole song – a five-minute sprawl with a fade-in: suggesting it was even longer – hangs on a numbingly primitive one-bar riff in E that simply churns over and over, with no dynamics or variation of any kind. Only after each chorus does a second pattern emerge, repeating for four bars, before we're plunged back to the original motif again, guitar and bass pounding it out in unison. Rat, too, quashes his naturally improvisatory and dynamic impulses, mainly playing minor variants of a single pattern as loudly as possible throughout, deepening the hypnotic monotony.

Vanian's vocal further contributes to this monochrome effect. Rather than opt for more of the Iggy-inspired frenzy that enlivened 'Alone', here Vanian delivers James' misanthropic lines in an insistent, tremulous tone, clinging doggedly to just two notes, almost for the song's duration. Atypical of natural showman Vanian, this 'anti-rock' approach actually anticipates the vocal style that John Lydon would adopt for his arty post-Pistols collective, Public Image Ltd (a band which would later include none other than Lu Edmonds in its ranks).

Indeed, the droning, punishing quality of 'You Know' looks ahead to the dark, drawn-out experiments of PIL's second album, 'Metal Box' (1979). But whether Lydon had even heard the track, he would certainly never have acknowledged its influence. The song's relentless repetition is only broken by Lol Coxhill's saxophone, just before the two-minute mark. Coxhill – a respected free-jazz improviser and veteran of the late-1960s Canterbury scene (which also spawned one of the Captain's formative influences: Soft Machine) came in through James to mirror Stooges saxophonist Steve Mackay's *Funhouse* role, and proves himself more than up to the task. His soprano sax paints free-form abstractions over the unrelentingly-uniform canvas, with long, keening notes, frantic Coltrane-like 'sheets of sound', and wild overblown shrieks. There are further sax overdubs in the final minute, intensifying the cacophony as the track fades back out.

In many ways, 'You Know' was a commendably bold move. Rather than simply repeating a successful formula, the band chose to end the LP with an experiment, which was both audacious and remarkably prescient of the darker turn that some post-punk music would take in years to come (generally to far greater critical acclaim than The Damned ever enjoyed). On the other hand, it makes for a gruelling listen, missing the crucial spark of fun that had always been present in even the band's darkest moments, thus providing a downbeat ending to an album that started out so brightly. It's a sombre final statement from The Damned mark one. Luckily, the reconfigured Damned would find ways to expand their musical horizons whilst retaining that sense of anarchic fun and simultaneously manage to be commercially viable, as we shall see!

Machine Gun Etiquette (1979)

Personnel:
Dave Vanian: lead vocals
Captain Sensible: guitar, backing vocals, keyboards, bass
Algy Ward: Bass, backing vocals, guitar
Rat Scabies: Drums, backing vocals
Additional personnel:
Joe Strummer: backing vocals on 'Noise Noise Noise'; Handclaps on 'Machine Gun Etiquette'
Topper Headon: backing vocals on 'Noise Noise Noise'
Henry Badowski: backing vocals on 'Noise Noise Noise'
Paul Simonon: handclaps on 'Machine Gun Etiquette'
Recorded at Sound Suite, Wessex Studios, The Workhouse Studios, Utopia Studios, SGS Studios and Chalk Farm Studios
Produced by: Roger Armstrong and The Damned
Record label: Chiswick
Released: 2 November 1979
Highest UK chart position: 31
Length: 35:28
Current edition: Chiswick Records 2007 CD/2014 LP reissue

The Damned weren't gone for long. Although their initial incarnation effectively ended in February 1978 when Brian James announced his intention to quit, they didn't officially disband until their farewell gig at the Rainbow on 8 April. Free from the musical straitjacket that punk had become for him, James went on to tread an idiosyncratic post-punk path, initially with Tanz der Youth, then in the 1980s finding commercial success with Lords Of The New Church: a supergroup of sorts, featuring Dead Boys' Stiv Bators, and members of Sham 69 and The Barracudas.

The other Damned members also threw themselves into new projects, with Rat forming hard-edged power-pop combo, The White Cats, and Sensible playing for a time with The Softies (with whom he recorded his fan-favourite cover of 'Jet Boy Jet Girl'), before forming the psych-pop tinged King with Wreckless Eric's Henry Badowski. Vanian, meanwhile, was rumoured to be working with pre-punk art-popsters, Doctors of Madness, but this never amounted to anything.

By August – after a few gigs and a couple of promising Peel sessions – both Rat and Captain's ventures were fizzling out. Discussions of a possible reunion began, with Vanian, Scabies and Sensible all onboard. Although Rat had left the band first, it was James who'd instigated the eventual break-up, and no one had been in touch with him since. With Sensible keen to move over to guitar (his first instrument), and all members eager to flex their developing songwriting muscles, it was tacitly agreed that their erstwhile leader would not be invited back.

Initially billed as Les Punks, and then The Doomed – for fear of incurring the wrath of Brian James: the presumed owner of the name (He wasn't bothered) – the band began to play a few gigs. Motorhead's Lemmy – a friend whose musical influence would creep into some of the band's more frenetic new material – temporarily filled Sensible's vacated bass position; followed by Henry Badowski, who might've been a keeper, were it not for a personality clash with Rat, culminating in some roadside fisticuffs. Finally, they settled on Alasdair 'Algy' Ward – formerly of then-London-based Aussie punk pioneers, The Saints – and by the start of 1979, were ready to get back to business as The Damned.

Significantly, this entailed an immediate return to the chaos and self-destructive behaviour which had contributed to their break-up in the first place: stumbling through shows in a blur of coke, speed and booze, leaving a trail of demolished instruments, dressing rooms and hotels in their wake. Almost as soon as he joined, Ward felt alienated from his new colleagues (who weren't exactly the most welcoming bunch), dealing with this by hitting the bottle extra hard, often barely able to stand by showtime.

Considering this apparent determination to sabotage themselves, it's a miracle that the band were capable of generating any new material at all, let alone anything as magnificent as the 'Love Song' single, which emerged in April 1979, reaching number 20 in the UK charts. The powerful, supremely catchy A-side – backed with the boisterous 'Noise Noise Noise' and a brooding rocker titled 'Suicide' – showed that the reformed Damned were a force to be reckoned with, capable of matching the attitude and energy of their earlier incarnation, while considerably broadening their musical horizons. The late-September release of the 'Smash It Up' single reinforced this impression: another perfect marriage of punk aggression and anthemic pop hooks, which – backed with Rat's bouncy novelty number, 'Burglar' – became another well-deserved top 40 hit, despite Radio One banning it for its potential to incite an uprising!

Machine Gun Etiquette came together in piecemeal fashion, with sessions recorded at various studios over a number of months, culminating in an August 1979 stint at Wessex Studios, where The Clash were also working, completing their similarly genre-redefining masterpiece, *London Calling*. Any residual ill-feeling between the two bands, lingering from the competitive, cliquey early punk days, had evaporated, and the two groups got on well, with three-quarters of The Clash ending up contributing backing vocals and handclaps to The Damned's record.

The Damned handled production themselves, along with Roger Armstrong – head of their new label, Chiswick – who also had, somewhat reluctantly, ended up managing them: surely one of the most thankless tasks in rock. With former principal songwriter James out of the picture – and four eager but relatively inexperienced writers contributing instead – the album's material arrived in a haphazard fashion, drawing on songs written for the White Cats and King, welcoming contributions from outside writers, and even taking in an MC5 cover. Yet somehow, against all odds, the assembled oddments cohered into an utterly convincing whole: a record which, in a changing punk landscape, affirmed The Damned's position at the very top of the heap, whilst pointing to several potential new musical directions that the James-era band (and most of their peers) wouldn't have dreamed of approaching.

The original front cover shows the boys at large on a New York City street, in their respective finery: Dave in vampiric black, the Captain in ludicrous all-over dayglo mohair, Algy the textbook rocker in denim and leather, and Rat looking surprisingly spiffy in a light blue blazer. The rear cover collage captures more of the band's anarchic spirit: in front of a backdrop of collapsing buildings, Rat demolishes his kit, wielding a cymbal stand like a weapon; Algy pounds his bass, legs splayed in full Ramones 'power stance'; and a Hawaiian-shirt-clad Sensible plays his guitar while sprawled on his back. Vanian, meanwhile – unrecognisable in a Count Orlok mask – lies flat-out, staring straight up, dead to the world. The inner sleeve features a madcap cartoon strip, giving a guide to the 'Smash It Up (Part 2)' chord shapes, which not only illustrated the band's sense of humour but presumably helped many an aspiring young punk play along with a record that reached well beyond the genre's expected simple three-chord thrash.

Machine Gun Etiquette was a respectable hit, receiving generally positive reviews, although some critics were determined to remain unimpressed: *Melody Maker*'s Paolo Hewitt prissily referring to the band as 'a tasteless joke'. Nevertheless, the album has only grown in stature and is now generally recognised as a terrific outpouring of creativity, taking in 1950s B-movies, 1960s pop, psychedelia, Detroit proto-punk and more – melding them into one of the greatest punk albums ever made, and one of the finest records produced by a British rock band, full stop.

'Love Song' (Rat Scabies / Captain Sensible / Dave Vanian / Algy Ward)

As the needle hits the groove, veteran Lancastrian actor John Howarth – best known as *Coronation Street*'s Albert Tatlock – asks, 'Ladies and gentlemen, 'ow do?': sounding like an easy-going Northern working men's club compere introducing the evening's entertainment.

What follows, however, is no easy-listening cabaret, as the band launches into the megalithic tension-building overture that begins 'Love Song' (The single version skips straight to the famous bass riff). Slow and deliberate – the rhythm section with a weight and a swing recalling early Black Sabbath – they churn through the chords, while Sensible loudly announces his arrival as guitarist with a searing lead break over a lot of excitable whooping and hollering, setting a celebratory tone for this spectacular comeback. After Vanian's off-mic yell of 'Hey man, what's happening?', Algy Ward proceeds to pound out a bass line every bit as iconic as that of the debut opener, 'Neat Neat Neat', from two years earlier. In this case, it's not so much the notes played, as the tone and aggression, that makes it so effective. The sound has a gravelly mid-range growl, edging into overdrive, and you can tell how forcefully Ward is playing: he's not merely picking the strings; he's knocking the hell out of them. Motorhead's Ian 'Lemmy' Kilmister is a palpable influence here: he favoured a similarly gnarly over-cranked bass tone, and many of Motorhead's best-known early songs were founded on fierce signature bass lines and galloping proto-thrash drums. Though often pigeonholed as a heavy metal act, Motorhead were always really more a fast, dirty rock 'n' roll band and certainly more punk-adjacent than such contemporary metal acts as, say, Judas Priest. By incorporating the ''Head's heaviness and speed into their sound, The Damned neatly one-upped the harder-edged second wave punk bands who'd come to the fore during their hiatus (U.K. Subs, Stiff Little Fingers et al.), while inadvertently laying the groundwork for the even more extreme acts yet to emerge (GBH, Discharge, and The Exploited, from whom this third wave acquired its retrospectively-applied 'UK82' moniker). Ward's scotch-for-breakfast lifestyle and determination to crank his amplifier to unrecordably deafening levels meant that little of his playing actually made it onto the album – Sensible overdubbing the majority of tracks – but with the 'Love Song' intro, he made his indelible mark on punk history.

A cascading drum fill and a shout of 'Go!' set us off at a ferocious pace, with more Sensible guitar heroism, before we settle into the verse. As with most of the Brian James-era material, the vocal line is constructed from simple pentatonic phrases: bluesy rather than melodic, and pitched somewhere in the middle of Vanian's vocal range, highlighting a growing confidence and warmth of tone. The lyrics are a delight, sardonically playing with pop cliches and conventions. 'I'll be the ticket if you're my collector / I've got the fare if you're my inspector', deadpans Vanian, before the chorus breaks in with a bright C major chord and a bold, chiming melody betraying a strong mid-1960s pop influence. The lyrics here – 'Just for you, here's a love song / And it makes me glad to say, it's been a lovely day, and it's okay' – may be the finest slice of satirical pop song banality since The Turtles' 'Eleanor' (1968) and its chorus hook, 'You're my pride and joy, etcetera'.

Although all the album's songs are credited equally to the band members (plus any outside writers who may have contributed), most were written largely by a single member. In this case, the Captain was largely responsible (with some input from Rat), and most of the hallmarks that would come to define his writing are immediately apparent, from the effortless sense of melody to the lyrical wit, teetering on the cusp of silliness; even down to the sneaky rail travel references (Sensible being an avid trainspotter when not wreaking punk havoc). The 'Love Song' single earned the band a memorable appearance on *Top of the Pops*; as an album opener, it laid down the gauntlet for all of their contemporaries, surpassing their earlier achievements and setting the bar for all punk to come.

'Machine Gun Etiquette' (Rat Scabies / Captain Sensible / Dave Vanian / Algy Ward)
If 'Love Song' left us breathless, the band had no intention of offering any respite. Another off-mic shout of 'Go!' spurs us straight back into a blistering thrash tempo for this savage riposte to the band's doubters, naysayers and critics (and there were many!). 'I remember what you said / Don't you wish that we were dead?' bellows Vanian, over a rumble of bass, with Sensible's guitar edging into feedback, threatening to spill out of control. After each line, an angry gang vocal bark of 'Second time around' affirms that The Damned have been granted another chance, and they intend to prove all their detractors wrong this time. The song seems so perfectly tailored to The Damned's renaissance that it's surprising to learn that Rat actually wrote it considerably earlier: for his post-break-up project, The White Cats, who recorded a version entitled 'Second Time Around', for a John Peel session.

Listening to that earlier recording, we can tell that – while most of the building blocks are in place – The Damned affected crucial changes to make the song their own. Firstly, the Captain's main guitar hook is absent from The White Cats' version: a simple three-note descending figure, played in octaves over a root note of F#, it serves to add a little depth to a song that's otherwise rather limited harmonically and melodically, and its sustained notes provide a nice contrast to the urgently-bubbling-over rhythm section. Secondly, on *Machine Gun Etiquette*, the original defiant-but-vague lyrics have been reworked to offer a completely on-the-nose commentary on the band's return. 'Now it's time for you to see what the love song did for me', gloats Vanian, as the band bask in their newfound success, thumbing their noses at those who wrote them off. Finally, The White Cats' recording, while still uptempo, takes a comparatively relaxed approach, with a driving swing reminiscent of Iggy Pop's 'Lust For Life' (1977). By the time The Damned get their hands on the song, that swing has been supplanted by a devastatingly relentless forward momentum, broken only by a brief, pummelling quarter-time breakdown section, in which Sensible's guitar motif resurfaces over massed clapping hands and stomping feet, courtesy of members of The Clash popping in from the studio next door.

At just 1:49, there's not a second wasted in this aptly-retitled track: a lean, brutal blast of prototypical hardcore, capturing The Damned at their most defiant and unrepentant.

'I Just Can't Be Happy Today' (Rat Scabies / Captain Sensible / Dave Vanian / Algy Ward / Giovanni Dadamo)
Having firmly established their credentials as the hardest, fastest punks on the block, with the LP's opening brace of tracks, 'I Just Can't Be Happy Today' allows the band to explore a different aspect of their sound, plunging into moody, atmospheric territory only hinted at on previous releases. After the guitar-heavy attack of the album's opening salvo, the keyboard-driven sound

here provides a welcome contrast, with the Captain making great use of a Vox Continental organ: the distinctive signature sound heard on such pop classics as The Doors' 'Light My Fire' (1967) and ? and the Mysterians' '96 Tears' (1966). No previous Damned recording had featured keyboards, and indeed, the punk movement as a whole had tended to shun them due to their unseemly association with the prog excesses of the likes of Rick Wakeman and Keith Emerson. The only notable UK band to buck the trend was the tricky-to-classify Stranglers, whose David Greenfield defied punk orthodoxy by not only playing keyboards but also proudly sporting a moustache! Similarly unconcerned with the judgements of punk's tastemakers, The Damned's embracing of keyboards was a clear nod to the psychedelic garage band influence that had always underpinned their music and which would become increasingly apparent in the years to come.

The song begins with a catchy guitar and bass riff, using the Mixolydian (major scale with a flattened 7th) mode over a droning E root note. Many pop songs from the mid-1960s onwards used this mode to create a slightly Indian feel – for example, The Kinks' 'See My Friends' (1965) and The Beatles' 'Getting Better' (1967) – and its use here effectively evokes that era of pop-psychedelia. From this intro, we're swept into the chorus, Vanian crooning the title, a dramatic shift to minor tonality and a sinister ascending chord sequence reflecting the mournful mood.

The intro riff returns for the verse, as the lyrics explain the narrator's sadness – he lives in a society in which enjoyment is forbidden, so he 'just can't be happy today', by law! 'There's no feeling fine without being fined', as one memorable piece of wordplay explains it. The lyrics – partly written by Giovanni Dadamo of the delightfully named Snivelling Shits – are an evocative mix of dark fantasy and equally dark satire. There are no specific references to real-world events, but Margaret Thatcher had assumed the UK premiership in May 1979, and many listeners may have drawn their own parallels.

A spoken-word middle-eight section heaps on the alarming detail ('They're closing the schools, they're burning the books / The church is in ruins, the priests hang on hooks'), with Vanian's delivery increasingly hysterical as the band, raises a tumultuous din behind him. The following organ solo feels like the sun momentarily breaking through the clouds. This sweetly-melodic section in G major was lifted from 'My Baby Don't' Care' (by Sensible's short-lived project, King), a slice of radiant sunshine pop which is practically the antithesis of 'I Just Can't Be Happy Today', yet the juxtaposition works remarkably well. A final verse introduces the rebellious streak one might expect from The Damned: a band not renowned for their respect for authority – 'Ignore all those fools / They don't understand we make our own rules'. After an extended chorus, the song fades with some catchy backing vocal 'woah's. Released as a single in November 1979 – backed with an entertaining Lemmy-powered cover of The Sweet's 'Ballroom Blitz', and the extremely silly Chas and Dave-ish novelty, 'The Turkey Song' – 'I Just Can't Be Happy Today' climbed to a modest peak of 46 in the UK. But its beautifully crafted dark pop marked a bold departure for the band, laying the groundwork for their direction in the new decade.

'Melody Lee' (Rat Scabies / Captain Sensible / Dave Vanian / Algy Ward)

As sources of inspiration for punk songs go, *Bunty* – a comic for girls, published from 1958 to 2001, offering a feminine counterpart to the stiff-upper-lip heroism of the similarly long-running boys' title, *Eagle* – is about as unlikely as they come. Nevertheless, Sensible – ever the wide-eyed child, with a fascination for the quaintly English – was an avid reader. His particular favourite *Bunty* series was 'Melody Lee – A Dancer She'll Be', which ran from June 1977 to October 1978, and told the rather mawkish tale of a young girl abandoned by her parents, who yearns for a career in ballet. Somehow, from this source material, the band found inspiration for one of their catalogue's most enigmatic and evocative songs.

It opens with a slow, lushly-romantic piano theme, utterly unlike anything The Damned had ever recorded before. Just as the listener is relaxing into the luxuriant melody, there's a startlingly abrupt cut; the same chords and melody now suddenly played and sung by the full band at maximum punk velocity and volume. The lyrics are a series of cryptic phrases and images ('A broken mind and a broken dream', 'Your life was cruel, they called it art') which (perhaps mercifully) don't refer directly to the comic strip, but which combine to create an elliptical narrative of a girl on a mysterious, and possibly dangerous, quest. In the booklet accompanying the 25th-anniversary reissue of *Machine Gun Etiquette*, Sensible claims that this intriguing, surprisingly poetic tapestry of images and allusions was actually pieced together from phrases taken directly from the *Bunty* pages. However, several internet sources who have checked the comic issues report that none of the lyric lines appear therein, so we can assume this was a cheeky bit of myth-making on the Captain's part. In a separate interview – given to John Robb for his excellent book, *Punk: An Oral History* – Sensible attributes the song to Vanian, which possibly makes more sense.

The band's playing is fearsome throughout, with some wonderfully elastic phrasing from Rat, and a rather Brian James-like solo from Sensible – a frenzied Chuck-Berry-on-speed assault, spiralling off into chaos – which is preceded by another Vanian cry of 'Go!'. It may just be coincidence that this rallying cry has cropped up in three of the first four songs here, but it perfectly epitomises the sense of urgency and powerful forward-momentum driving the whole album; for all their wild antics in public and on the road, The Damned aren't messing around on this record.

The whole thing is over in a flash, slamming to a halt just beyond the two-minute mark. In that time, it has perfectly illustrated the band's newfound ability to meld tough, uncompromising punk with a haunting melody, sophisticated harmony and unexpectedly deft lyric writing. 'Melody Lee' was never a single but has become a fan favourite – a stand-out track on an outstanding album.

'Antipope' (Rat Scabies / Captain Sensible / Dave Vanian / Algy Ward / Phillip Burns)

Another song that came from an outside source, 'Antipope' (or 'Anti Pope', as it's sometimes rendered) was written by the Captain's brother, Phil Burns, and originally performed by his band, The Cowards. It then became part of King's repertoire, recorded by them for a 1978 John Peel session, before eventually cropping up in Damned sets as they were casting around for post-reunion album material. Listening to King's recording, it's clear that 'Antipope' was complete and fully realised before The Damned got hold of it, although they did some rearranging – upping the tempo (which makes the already-wordy lyrics especially tongue-twisting for poor Vanian), and adding a different, slightly more structured instrumental breakdown. Whether these changes warranted the entire band claiming writing credit is debatable, but that's another matter!

The song itself is a playful but pointed take-down of organised religion – and especially Catholicism – based around a punchy two-chord vamp. The verse lyrics have a sense of mischief very much in keeping with the band's character. Our protagonist is going to church, 'But I don't mean to pray / I'm gonna nick the collection plate'. The mischief continues, as later our narrator spreads a rumour that 'The vicar's a transvestite / With a fetish for robes and gowns'. However, this light-heartedness is balanced through harder-hitting commentary, as the chorus rails against 'plain ignorant' churchgoers: 'So many people are weak and then have to seek answers from the pedlars of hope / I should know, I used to go there myself.' It's fairly vehement, becoming even more so in the final verse, which proclaims 'Religion doesn't mean a thing / It's just another way of being right-wing': quite a change for a band who just two years earlier were writing songs proclaiming their apolitical stance. While The Damned would always be worlds away from the street-level sloganeering of many post-Clash punks, with Brian James out of the picture, and Sensible in particular becoming more engaged with the issues of the day, a certain sociopolitical consciousness was beginning to assert itself in the band's work.

Following another fine Captain solo, the song breaks down into an atmospheric instrumental section, with maracas, claves and congas playing an Afro-Cuban rhythm: the 'Bo Diddley' beat, beloved of rock 'n' rollers since time immemorial. There are definite echoes of the Rolling Stones' 'Sympathy For The Devil' (1968), which, given the irreligious subject matter, is probably deliberate, as Sensible builds layers of stinging feedback guitar and melodic bass runs over the wall of percussion before Rat's rattling triplet snare roll lurches into the final verse.

Though certainly not the first explicitly anti-religious punk song, 'Antipope' is an early and powerful example, setting a precedent for such spectacular blasphemies as Charged GBH's 'The Prayer Of A Realist' (1982) and The Dead Kennedys' terrific *In God We Trust Inc.* EP (1981): the latter of which included 'Moral Majority' ('God must be dead if you're alive!') and the self-explanatory 'Religious Vomit'. 'Antipope' shows us that, for the first time, The Damned had made an album where their impactful music matched their provocative and intelligent lyrics.

'These Hands' (Rat Scabies / Captain Sensible / Dave Vanian, / Algy Ward)
This delightfully twisted little number fully embraced the horror imagery only implicit on earlier Damned records. In lurching waltz-time, the bass, organ and guitar blend to mimic a fairground calliope, steaming out of control as the song progresses. Over this unsettling backdrop, Vanian's deep baritone croon sets the scene, creepy whispered phrases occasionally highlighting. The character is a 'demented circus clown', who, spurned and mocked by the object of his affection, now dreams of revenge, breaking into increasingly hysterical laughter as he imagines himself squeezing the life from her: 'I find I am laughing at you / And you are turning blue.' The lunatic cackling and spooky ambience intensify until abruptly curtailed at 1:49 by a cry of 'Stop laughing!'. In the ensuing hush, we hear two sets of footsteps moving through the stereo spectrum from the right. As they reach the far left, a female voice gasps in surprise and a male voice chuckles sadistically.

This is pure theatre, and Vanian plays his role with relish. In the eerie waltz accompaniment, there are echoes of the sinister fairgrounds of horror classics such as the film *Carnival of Souls* (1962) or Ray Bradbury's novel, *Something Wicked This Way Comes* (1962), while the 'happy-on-the-outside, murderous-on-the-inside' narrator may owe something to the Alice Cooper song, 'Years Ago', from *Welcome to My Nightmare* (1975), with its first-person depiction of a fractured psyche. About as far from any textbook definition of punk rock as you could get, 'These Hands' represents an aspect of the band that would soon come to the fore, eventually forming the basis of their whole identity.

'Plan 9 Channel 7' (Rat Scabies / Captain Sensible / Dave Vanian / Algy Ward)
If 'These Hands' is the first Damned song to fully delve into Dave Vanian's fascination with horror, 'Plan 9 Channel 7' focuses on another of his abiding preoccupations: the glamour and allure of Hollywood's bygone age. The song addresses the unconsummated relationship between Maila Nurmi – the actress who found fame as late-night TV hostess and B-movie star, Vampira – and James Dean. The 'Plan 9' of the title refers to Ed Wood's legendarily-inept sci-fi shocker, *Plan 9 From Outer Space* (1956, released 1959), which starred Nurmi, alongside another Vanian influence, Bela Lugosi, in his final role. In

keeping with the subject, Vanian's lyrics are positively cinematic, telling the story through a series of striking images. The song has a bold, unabashed romanticism, in stark contrast to the terse, austere approach many of The Damned's punk contemporaries took.

The first line immediately puts us in the picture: 'She plays her mouth into a smile / And offers that he stay a while'. Later we're told, 'She lays a wreath of lilies on his grave / His flame gone, along with the love he never gave', as a backing vocal sings a counter-melody, repeating the phrase 'Come and join me'. In verse one, this is a reference to a postcard Nurmi reportedly sent to Dean, but by verse two, it has transposed into Dean's voice, beckoning from beyond the grave (Nurmi claimed to have made psychic contact with Dean's spirit, following his untimely passing).

In keeping with the words' filmic feel, there's a sweeping, widescreen quality to the music: a marked contrast to the linear muscularity of the album's more straight-ahead punk material. Opening with dramatic guitar chords of Em and C – made dissonant by the addition of a B flat, bending up towards B natural – the verses settle on an F major chord, a portentous rising A minor figure capping each line. As the closely-observed verses give way to the broader focus of the bridge and chorus ('Hollywood babbles on'), Vanian's single lead line becomes double-tracked, giving a broader stereo spread, and the tone of the song changes with a shift to G major and a wash of organ chords, Sensible's guitar playing a breezy melody, counter to the vocal.

Consisting of only two brief verses, the narrative is only lightly sketched and hinted at, preserving a sense of mystery and allowing the listener's imagination to fill in any gaps. With Vanian imploring us to 'Step into the night', the remainder of the song's five minutes is given over to an extended instrumental outro, during which Sensible's guitar soars impressively, joined by Vanian's wholly-unexpected vocal falsetto, oddly recalling Ian Gillan's vocal gymnastics on Deep Purple's rock epic, 'Child In Time' (1970). Ultimately, 'Plan 9 Channel 7' is another crowning glory – a superbly crafted gothic masterpiece, highlighting Vanian's spectacular growth as a songwriter. Having made his inauspicious debut a mere two years earlier – co-authoring the utterly banal 'Your Eyes' – he was now producing work with a scope and nuance level far beyond the bounds of what most narrow 'punk' definitions would accept.

'Noise Noise Noise' (Rat Scabies / Captain Sensible / Dave Vanian / Algy Ward / Jennet Ward)

After the ambitious and sophisticated 'Plan 9 ... ', it's up to Rat to bring us back down to earth, and he does so with aplomb on this joyously gormless blast of yob rock. The lyrics – written with input from Rat's then-girlfriend, Jennet Ward – follow the narrator through his day as a suburban punk: listening to records, arguing with his parents, going to the pub, playing a gig at the local church hall and upsetting the vicar in the process (Between 'I Just Can't Be Happy Today', 'Antipope' and this track, members of the clergy are given a pretty rough time).

40

This day-in-the-life approach – and the boot boy gang chorus backing vocals (aided again by members of The Clash) – draw parallels with Sham 69: the self-proclaimed 'cockney cowboys' and forerunners of the 'Oi!' skinhead punk movement, whose similarly-themed concept LP, *That's Life*, had been a hit the previous year. The words are enjoyable doggerel, bursting with daft couplets – 'I kick the dog, I kick the cat / Insult my mum, insult my dad' – their crudity perfectly matching the chorus' anti-artistry rallying cry: 'Noise is for heroes / Leave the music for zeroes!'

This is a bold restatement of the early-Damned's single-minded devotion to simple, raw rock 'n' roll, chaos and destruction; but it doesn't ring quite true, coming, as it does, part-way through an album already revealing musicianship far beyond the confines of basic 1976-model punk rock. Even the arrangement here packs some musical surprises: resisting the temptation to simply blast through the track with power chords *ala* Johnny Ramone, Sensible plays the track almost entirely in single-note lines, from the surprisingly-fiddly main riff onwards, even allowing his two tracks to fall into Thin Lizzy-style harmony in verse two. Aside from this, the verses have deliberately spare instrumentation: the Captain's guitar ringing out into feedback, and Rat's usually busy percussive onslaught pared down to a simple 'boom-thwack' of kick, snare and floor tom. This leaves only the bass (overdubbed by Sensible) to provide harmonic underpinning for Vanian's vocal, creating a quiet/LOUD dynamic of the type that Nirvana and their grunge brethren later popularised. Incidentally, the song's earlier recording on the 'Love Song' 45 B-side has an almost identical arrangement, yet the dynamic contrast is less marked, due entirely to Algy's huge, obnoxious bass sound, filling up all available mix space. All in all, although 'Noise Noise Noise' is perfectly fine on its own terms, it feels a little weak and slapdash compared to the other material on offer here and represents an attitude the band had already started to outgrow.

'Looking At You' (Michael Davis / Wayne Kramer / Fred Smith / Dennis Thompson / Rob Tyner)

Having paid homage to The Stooges on the debut album's 'I Feel Alright', The Damned now turned their attention to Iggy and the gang's Detroit compatriots, peers and mentors, MC5. 'Looking At You' made its first appearance in a Damned set at the September 1978 Les Punks reunion, with Lemmy guesting on bass, a two-chord song being just the ticket when assembling a set on minimal rehearsal time! The song itself – a curious account of a singer being incapacitated on the bandstand by glimpsing of a mystery blonde in the audience – goes back to the very early MC5 days: a live version from the *'66 Breakout* album revealing that it started life as a mid-tempo harmonica-driven blues. By the time MC5 recorded it for a 1968 single, it had dramatically changed into a pounding, fuzzed-up rocker in a blown-out recording that still sounds astonishing. MC5 re-recorded the song with producer John Landau for the 1970 *Back in the USA* album: a clean, tight, punchy version that is the best known and forms the basis for The Damned's cover.

Naturally, The Damned's rendition is considerably accelerated, opening with an abrupt machine-gun snare roll, straight into the insistent E to D pattern that repeats, unchanging throughout the track's five-plus minutes. It's pretty simple, and keeping the listener engaged over the entire track, required a powerhouse performance. For all their punk rock influence, MC5 were dauntingly great musicians, and it takes a brave and/or foolish band to cover an MC5 song and expect to live up to the original. Luckily for us, The Damned are both brave 'and' foolish, and terrific players to boot.

Scabies is in buoyant form, driving the track along at a fierce clip, carefully steering the dynamics from a roar to a whisper and back, throwing in gymnastic fills along the way. Dave Vanian doesn't quite have the strident upper vocal range of MC5's Rob Tyner but does well to even fit the lyrics in at this pace! Meanwhile, Sensible delivers an absolute masterclass: not only single-handedly recreating the fabled Wayne Kramer/Fred 'Sonic' Smith guitar partnership (which Brian James tried but failed to achieve with Lu Edmonds), but also playing the bass part, guiding the ebb and flow in a way that the talented-but-heavy-handed Algy Ward could not. All of *Machine Gun Etiquette* is a *tour de force* for Sensible, but it is here that he proves himself to be the original punk generation's greatest lead guitarist by a considerable margin: as accomplished as any of the classic rock era's celebrated heroes, but with a fire, spontaneity and intensity that is entirely punk.

'Liar' (Rat Scabies / Captain Sensible / Dave Vanian / Algy Ward)

Of all the album's songs, 'Liar' is the one that comes closest to the band's original sonic template; although, curiously, it was written by Algy Ward: the one member not part of the band's initial incarnation. It's punchy, obnoxious-but-daft knockabout fun of the first order, Ward's stampeding bass pushing it along: for once actually making it to the finished recording. There's no shortage of punk songs titled 'Liar': The Sex Pistols' 1977 effort being perhaps the best known. However, rather than accusing an unspecified 'you' of being a liar, Algy's song flips the script, with the narrator cheerfully celebrating his own dishonesty. This gives Vanian the opportunity to play the villain, which, of course, he does splendidly, delivering even the silliest lines with a gleeful leer: 'I send your mum to bed to find if your sister's frigid'. Sensible reins in his more experimental side, playing it straight 1977 style, with propulsive 8th-notes and a brief, gnarled solo, very much in the Brian James mould.

It's not quite punk-by-numbers though, as a couple of interesting and unusual things are happening amidst the familiar racket: the chord structure takes a jarring leap from verse to chorus, stopping the listener from getting too cosy; the mix too, is slightly unusual, with Rat's huge-sounding drums very much to the fore, especially in the post-middle-eight breakdown. This section provides rare insight into swing and dance band drummers' formative influence on

Rat's playing style: heavily indebted to Gene Krupa's iconic intro to the Benny Goodman Orchestra's big band classic, 'Sing Sing Sing' (1937). It's a nice touch, elevating this fine example of the raw, snotty rock 'n' roll The Damned built their career on – but a style they would come to visit less and less frequently.

'Smash It Up (Part 1)' (Rat Scabies / Captain Sensible / Dave Vanian / Algy Ward)

Going by the title, you might expect 'Smash It Up' to find the band at their most direct and aggressive. The reality is more intriguing. The 'Smash It Up' single is actually the second movement of a four-part suite: an ambitious and atypically-punk concept. Parts three and four were not completed in the end (Ace records finally issued a CD single including Sensible's demo versions of these in 2004), but this thoughtful and atmospheric instrumental, was.

Based around a series of ringing guitar arpeggios, the track builds gently, Sensible's clean, reverb-drenched guitar joined first by some tasteful bass (Sensible again), and then an admirably-restrained Rat. The main guitar figure's haunting quality comes from ringing open strings, creating almost folk-sounding suspended notes (The opening chord is A major with an additional suspended 4th and a dominant 7th). Clearly, we're not in power chord punk territory here, and the track owes more to Sensible's enduring fondness for prog and art rock than it does to anything remotely punky. Taken out of context, it sounds closer to Pink Floyd or Rush than The Stooges or New York Dolls. It also appears to anticipate the post-rock movement, which emerged from the artier end of the 1980s US hardcore scene: the measured tempos and chiming guitars of Slint's 1991 magnum opus, *Spiderland*, are strikingly reminiscent of 'Smash It Up (Part 1)'.

The track waxes and wanes, gradually gathering pace, eventually arriving at G major, for a brief jangling guitar chords section that foreshadows part two. At the 1:55 mark, part one draws to a close with a mournful E minor chord, leaving behind a wistful mood that swiftly evaporates as a skilful cross-fade introduces the next section.

'Smash It Up' (Rat Scabies / Captain Sensible / Dave Vanian / Algy Ward)

Part 2 (simply listed as 'Smash It Up' on the original album rear) immediately picks up the tempo. However, while the title and lyrics express a familiar strain of punk rebellion, the sound – all sharp, clean guitars and '96 Tears'-style garage band organ – is closer to mid-1960s beat group pop, albeit played with thoroughly punky drive and aggression. Part one's dark, enigmatic ambience has been swept away, leaving a bright, uptempo number in G major, with a sing-along melody, simple chord progressions, and an irresistible chanting chorus. As Sensible's inner-sleeve cartoon – 'Mr God Awful Ugly' – demonstrates, the main guitar riff is characterised through a constantly ringing open G, droning throughout the song, creating an almost Byrds-like folk rock feel. This was unheard of in the punk rock world of 1979 when Johnny Ramone-style barre chords were strictly the order of the day. However, as the 1980s wore on, a similar reliance on open-string drones could be heard in the work of such influential players as Bob Mould (Husker Du), Brian Baker (Dag Nasty, Bad Religion) and Billy Joe Armstrong (Green Day): it would be a surprise if the Captain's playing here had not made an impact. Another trick, unexpectedly borrowed from folk music, can be heard in the slightly unusual verse phrase lengths. In folk song arrangements, it is common for the singer to take a couple of beats of rest after each lyric line – partly to let the words sink in and partly to gather breath – and that's exactly what The Damned do here. The change is subtle, but it gives each line a little more weight, reinforcing the impression that we're listening to a sort of modern folk song – an anthem of popular uprising.

So what are we meant to be rising against and smashing up? The rabble-rousing lyrics apparently concerned the BBC enough for them to ban the single from Radio 1, which undoubtedly hurt its chart performance (though it still reached a respectable 35). Looking at the words now, it's hard to see what they were worried about. By 1979, Crass were building a following with their radical anarcho-punk, writing songs advocating actual political anarchy, and backing up their words with their non-hierarchical communal lifestyle at Dial House in Epping. In comparison, The Damned are not calling on us to smash the state. Instead, 'Smash It Up' is essentially a defiant but tongue-in-cheek rallying cry against faddish conformity. 'People call me villain, it's such a shame / Maybe it's my clothes must be to blame,' sings Vanian, who has dressed as a vampire for his entire career. He might be onto something!

The track peaks with the middle eight, as yobbish gang vocals chant 'Smash it up!' while Vanian picks-off targets one at a time: 'Krishna burgers', 'Glastonbury hippies' and 'Pints of frothy lager' are all in the firing line. Lyricist, Sensible – a cask ale fanatic – had yet to embrace vegetarianism: a change he would make later after visiting the aforementioned Dial House commune. Amusingly, The Damned would eventually play to the 'Glastonbury hippies', performing on the Avalon Stage at the 2003 festival, where they closed their set with – you guessed it – 'Smash It Up'!

After a final chorus, the tempo slows to a woozy stagger, and the assembled crew sing a last refrain of 'Everybody's smashing things down', sounding for all the world like an after-hours pub sing-along. The track fades out and thus ends *Machine Gun Etiquette* – that is unless your stylus runs into the vinyl's final lock-groove, which plays the phrase 'Nibbled to death by an okapi' repeatedly until you lift the needle!

'Smash It Up' perfectly encapsulates the power, spirit and musicality of The Damned's second phase. The song is an essential part of every live Damned set, and also brought them to a new audience when a cover by Orange County's multiplatinum punks, The Offspring, featured on the soundtrack to Joel Schumacher's film, *Batman Forever* (1995). The Offspring would go on to play a further role in The Damned's story, as we shall see in due course.

The Black Album (1980)

Personnel:

David Vanian: vocals, harmonium on 'Curtain Call'

Captain Sensible: guitar, keyboards, lead vocals on 'Silly Kid's Games'

Paul Gray: bass

Rat Scabies: drums, 12-string guitar and backing vocals on 'Drinking About My Baby'

Additional personnel:

Hans Zimmer: synthesizers on 'The History Of The World (Pt. 1)' and 'Lively Arts'

Ray Martinez: trumpet on 'Twisted Nerve'

Recorded at Rockfield Studios, mixed at Rockfield and Portland Recording Studios (studio tracks)

Live tracks recorded at Rock City Studios, Shepperton.

Produced by the Kings of Reverb (The Damned), except 'The History Of The World (Pt. 1)': produced by Hans Zimmer

Engineer: Hugh Jones

Record label: Chiswick (UK), IRS (USA – sides one and two only)

Release date: 3 November 1980

Highest UK chart position: 29

Current edition: 2005 Big Beat Records reissue with bonus tracks.

The Damned entered 1980 with real momentum. *Machine Gun Etiquette* had confirmed the viability of the reconfigured Brian James-less band, taking them to new creative heights and providing some solid commercial success to boot. They'd received a silver record for album sales; notched up TV appearances on both mainstream pop platform, *Top of the Pops*, and 'serious' showcase, *The Old Grey Whistle Test* (a memorably chaotic showing, well worth looking up on YouTube); and had toured the UK and the US. Obviously, this being The Damned, there were stumbling blocks: most notably the total breakdown of their already fractious relationship with bassist Algy Ward, leading to his sacking shortly after the conclusion of the American tour. Luckily, the band already had someone in mind: Paul Gray. Rat had been keen for the former Eddie and the Hot Rods bassist to join The Damned since the reunion, and now the timing was right. Gray could easily muster the power to handle the band's most aggressive material and also possessed the taste, musicality and melodic nous to compliment their rapidly broadening musical scope. Furthermore, he was a good match personality-wise, shared many common influences, and crucially, was an accomplished songwriter.

Initial recording sessions took place at Wessex Studios, where the previous album had been finished. But most of those tracks were not complete, serving as demos for what would become *The Black Album*, although a few songs did surface on a 7' single in France and Germany, giving an insight into the band's new direction. A surprisingly straight-ahead cover of the Jefferson Airplane's psych classic 'White Rabbit' was chosen as the A-side, Sensible enjoying the opportunity to stretch out with some expansive lead breaks, and Vanian gamely clambering to the very heights of his range to replicate Grace Slick's vocal. Only the drums added a slightly punky element, replacing the original's exotic flamenco-inspired rhythm with a more driving four-square beat. On the B-side, an intriguingly proggy instrumental titled 'Seagulls' continued exploring avenues that 'Smash It Up' had opened. But the real gem was 'Rabid (Over You)': a song combining punkish bluster, gothic melodrama and radio-friendly pop hooks, to terrific effect. Blending raw guitars with buzzing synths and a driving, metronomic rhythm giving it a Devo-like new wave quality, the song is an overlooked Damned classic, which promised great things for the album to come.

With Chiswick Records feeling confident following the success of *Machine Gun Etiquette*, the band were booked for three weeks at the legendary Rockfield residential studios in rural Wales, giving the band their first opportunity to concentrate completely on the recording process, away from the distractions of London. After swiftly firing label-appointed producer Alvin Clark, The Damned set about producing the album themselves, and – displaying a remarkable level of focus for such a notoriously chaotic group – completed within three weeks, sufficient music for three LP sides; one side entirely taken up by Vanian's heroically-ambitious 17-minute epic, 'Curtain Call'. In order to fill out the double album, they decided to include some live tracks, showcasing the revitalised Damned's onstage power. A show was arranged for fan club members, taking place at Shepperton Studios on 26 July, at the conclusion of a brief summer tour. Six songs were selected to complete the LP (these were later reissued as part of a whole album of the same show: the self-explanatory *Live Shepperton 1980* (Big Beat, 1982)).

The album title is a pun on The Beatles' self-titled 1968 LP, universally known as *The White Album*, and the parallels between the two are clear: both are hugely ambitious double sets, with individual members' songs expanding the bands' sound in a variety of directions (as with the previous Damned album, although all songs are credited to the entire band, most tracks were written by a single individual). The new album saw the band more fully embrace the dark, proto-gothic tone that emerged on 'These Hands' and 'Plan 9 Channel 7', so naturally, it became the 'Black' album. After some debate, they resisted the urge to parody The Beatles' sleeve by packaging the LP in plain black with just The Damned in embossed lettering, although the later single-LP reissue on Big Beat records did use this concept. Instead, the original cover – designed by Vanian – features a weathered plaque with the band name in twisting, demonic-looking script on a dark wall surrounded by gnarled branches and cobwebs. It looks like the entrance to a mausoleum in an old Hammer shocker, which is perfect for the spooky, theatrical tone of much of the record. The rear cover shows the band's illuminated faces surrounded by darkness, very much like the cover of *Queen II* and the 'Bohemian Rhapsody' promo video (1975, also partially recorded at Rockfield, incidentally). However, The Damned's image has an added air of menace, courtesy of the otherworldly purple glow suffusing the shot and a strange light appearing to emanate from the band members' eyes.

This bold double album statement was sold for the price of a single album (as was The Clash's similarly mould-breaking 1979 double set, *London Calling*), climbing to a healthy number 29 in the UK. However, the bargain price – though good for encouraging sales – did little to recover the high recording costs and myriad other expenses the band had run up (their penchant for wanton hotel-trashing didn't help matters), leaving them in a shaky financial situation with Chiswick Records – who, to give them their due, had been extremely supportive.

The music press were a little baffled by a band still generally perceived in narrow punk terms, producing an album of such depth and variety. But most reviews were at least cautiously impressed, with *Record Mirror* noting the band's 'metamorphosis from speedy young yobbos to acidic adults', and *Sounds* identifying Syd Barrett and The Beach Boys among the audible influences.

Like many of The Damned's records, *The Black Album* has only grown in stature, with *Louder Than War* magazine – in a review of the expanded reissue – describing it as 'The best album the late-'60s Who never made'. But many retrospectives still overlook this era of The Damned, instead highlighting the work of trendier post-punk contemporaries. But to those in the know, *The Black Album* stands as a true work of art, and in some respects, a Damned career peak.

'Wait for the Blackout' (David Vanian / Paul Gray / Rat Scabies / Captain Sensible / Billy Karloff)

A triumphant album opener, which effectively acts as a theme song for the album. The energy of the band's earlier material is still very much apparent, but instead of a proto-hardcore runaway train, there's a tight, controlled power – driving, but not racing. A great big hooky guitar riff in A introduces the track, with Sensible playing an immensely catchy melodic line over his open A, E and D strings. Scabies and Gray accent the chord changes before Rat's signature round-the-kit two-bar roll brings in the rhythm. Scabies has told interviewers that a hand injury hampered his playing on *The Black Album*, leaving him effectively one-handed, and, listening closely, there are moments where he may seem a little less ebullient than usual, although always serving the song perfectly. Nevertheless, his playing here certainly seems to be at its full-blooded, two-handed best, blending beautifully with Paul Gray's lithe and effortlessly melodic bass part. His playing is masterful, taking in pedal-tone drones, Motown grooves, high-up-the-neck chord voicings and John Entwistle-like fills. This frees Sensible from simply playing chords, allowing him to concentrate on chiming melodic figures and some nifty Indian raga infused leads (that Mixolydian mode again!) for a 1960s psych feel.

The song sounds like a classic Dave Vanian product but was actually co-written by Rat, the Captain, and the wonderfully-named Billy Karloff: a pal of Rat's and a member of The Extremes. Nevertheless, Vanian firmly stamps his personality on the track, his increasingly powerful baritone luring us into the darkness like a spooky Scott Walker. Vanian had actually begun to take professional vocal lessons, and while his voice had always been one of the band's most distinctive attributes, there's a newfound strength and assurance to his *Black Album* performances. The verses find his velvet tones beckoning the unsuspecting listener into his 'basement flat, no windows to see through', drawing us further into the inviting darkness and imploring us to 'Wait for the blackout, wait for the night'. The middle eight provides a brief oasis of calm, with a naïve, almost nursery-rhyme-sounding melody over gently-picked acoustic guitar chords and twinkling harmonics. Lest we should suspect any nefarious motives, our narrator here protests his innocence: 'In darkness, there is no sin / Light only brings the fear.' Naturally, we don't believe a word of it – Vanian's suave delivery is far too knowing to be anything other than roguish – and the illusion of calm is soon shattered, as the band works itself into a frenzy, a peal of bells adding to the general cacophony.

Musically and thematically, 'Wait for the Blackout' couldn't be a more perfect choice to open with. Although this is not a 'concept album' *per se*, by bookending the first three album sides with this track and 'Curtain Call', The Damned create the impression that the diverse material in-between is part of a coherent whole: unified by the band's gleeful embrace of their dark side. 'Wait for the Blackout' has become a Damned live set staple, and was notably covered by popular Chicago punks, Alkaline Trio, whose blend of pop melody, dark atmospherics and a crooning vocal style owes much to The Damned.

'Lively Arts' (David Vanian / Paul Gray / Rat Scabies / Captain Sensible)

An insistent drum rhythm cross-fades in from the previous song, the bass drum pulsing hard. Sensible's guitar strikes a thickly distorted and slightly phase-shifted chord, and seamlessly we're off into 'Lively Arts'. The verses settle into fairly traditional Damned territory, Sensible's chugging palm-muted power chords and Gray's muscular bass, conveying a punky attitude matching the lyric's snotty howl of class resentment. The chorus, however, moves in a wholly unexpected direction. The rhythm section continues in pummelling momentum, an elaborate neo-baroque orchestral synthesizer arrangement (courtesy of Hans Zimmer, later to make his name as a prolific and hugely successful film score composer) now supplanting the guitar. The faux-grandeur of soaring electronic trumpet lines and violin arpeggios carries through to the vocal, Vanian's voice layered in both baritone and falsetto tracks for a choral effect. This shift from down-to-earth rock to classical pomposity helps illustrate the lyric, in which our working-class narrator dreams of a life of leisure while cursing middle-class pretensions: ' ... and culture's just a bore when you're angry young and poor / And if I had my way, those idle rich would pay.' On one hand, this can be seen as a continuation of themes from songs like 'Noise Noise Noise' or 'Problem Child'; the band empathising with slobs, scoundrels and ne'er do wells everywhere, and favouring raw, dirty rock 'n' roll over any snobbish notions of artistry or sophistication. However, in this case, there is surely an element of self-parody or deliberate caricature creeping in: certainly, no one can deny the band their working-class roots (while many of their punk contemporaries came from extremely cosy backgrounds), but at the same time, they could hardly conceal their musical ambitions, which now stretched far beyond primitive early punk.

The two verses and choruses fly by in two minutes, the final minute given over to a duel between Sensible's snarling guitar and the beeps and buzzes of Zimmer's synths, while Rat keeps the almost mechanical-sounding rhythm, pounding away. Incidentally, with little audible evidence of cymbals, this may be one track that Rat played 'one-handed' due to injury. If so, the simple, driving kick and snare patterns fit the track very well, and it's hard to imagine it with Scabies' typically looser, busier playing style. Eventually, an ominous chromatic sequence of rising chords brings 'Lively Arts' to a dramatic close, the sense of continuity ushering us straight into the next song.

'Silly Kid's Games' (David Vanian / Paul Gray / Rat Scabies / Captain Sensible)

After a hard-hitting opening brace of songs, an uncharacteristically laid-back and bluesy acoustic 12-string guitar riff tells us we are now heading into distinctly more reflective territory. The subtlety at work here would've been unthinkable for earlier incarnations of The Damned, and the mix of influences on display owes more to classic rock and pop than to anything strictly punk: the witty, gently satirical lyrics and plaintive and very English lead vocal (Sensible on frontman duties for the first time), recall Ray Davies' contributions to The Kinks' run of great 1960s records; the accompaniment – all brisk acoustic rhythm guitar, tasteful electric leads, luxuriant Hammond B3 organ chords and nimble, lively rhythm section – is clearly indebted to The Who's Glyn Johns-produced early-1970s albums; and the middle eight's wordless vocal arrangement playfully parodies The Beach Boys, over a *Pachelbel's Canon*-style circle-of-fifths chord progression (a device later famously used on The Farm's 1990 hit, 'All Together Now').

The lyric finds our narrator dreaming of making his fortune, not through hard work or inspiration, but by appearing on a TV game show. Sensible manages to sneak in references to popular shows of the day: such as *3-2-1*, where unlucky losers would be awarded the show's mascot 'Dusty Bin' as a booby prize; and *The Generation Game*, wherein the list of potential prizes contestants were required to memorise to win, would inevitably include 'a cuddly toy'. The Captain also gets extra points for audacious use of rhyme, with the couplet, 'When I win all the loot, don't you have no fear / I'm going to take my hols in Kampuchea!' Interestingly, in the same year, San Francisco punk insurgents, The Dead Kennedys, also floated the idea of vacationing under the auspices of the Khmer Rouge on their classic, 'Holiday in Cambodia'. Whether The Damned hit on the same idea by coincidence or were making a deliberate reference, we may never know. A marked contrast to Vanian's always-theatrical presentation, the Captain's down-to-earth and unmannered vocal style, suits the lyric's knowing mundanity and 'Silly Kid's Games' – though not a top-tier Damned classic – is a beautifully crafted and highly entertaining slice of kitchen sink pop. As the song nears its end, the intro's bluesy 12-string returns, setting us up for yet another neat segue.

'Drinking About My Baby' (David Vanian / Paul Gray / Rat Scabies / Captain Sensible)

After 'Silly Kid's Games' key of A major, a solo piano passage leaves us in B, in the process creating a totally false expectation of the type of song to follow. Just as we're settling in, in anticipation of some brooding atmospherics, a bass slide punctures the mood, and the raunch and aggression of 'Drinking About My Baby' blind-sides us. With blazing guitar power chords and flying-off-the-handle drum fills, we're firmly back in old-school Damned territory here.

The song is constructed around a simple guitar riff oscillating between B to A, the end of each phrase landing on a D chord. Not only does this motif underpin both verse and chorus, but it exactly mirrors the vocal throughout. This could all get monotonous very quickly, but thankfully, a burst of jangly 12-string melody (played by Rat, the song's composer, interestingly) breaks up each verse, adding a touch of Searchers-like 1960s folk pop to proceedings: a dash of colour amidst the moody riffing.

In keeping with the music's fairly rudimentary nature, the lyric is somewhat perfunctory: the narrator loved his 'baby', lost her, and is now drinking to forget. But there is plenty to enjoy here: catchy harmonies, yet another searing Captain solo, and Gray's superb roving bass line. It's an exciting rock 'n' roll record, brilliantly played and skilfully produced, but compared to much of the album, it seems a tad unimaginative. While most of the songs were written especially for the album, 'Drinking About My Baby' originated a little earlier and was played live with Algy Ward (who hated it), which may partly explain why it doesn't quite sit comfortably with some of the other songs here.

'Twisted Nerve' (David Vanian / Paul Gray / Rat Scabies / Captain Sensible)

After a brief pause (the first since the album began), we are whisked back into the shadowy, cinematic territory so beloved of Dave Vanian. Gray's bass – given an otherworldly quality through lashings of reverb, tremolo and chorus effects – twangs out a menacing minor-key riff, instantly evoking spy-movie soundtracks, setting the tone for the song's oblique narrative: a creepy psychological murder mystery with added hints of John le Carre espionage thriller. The arrangement is stark and minimal, the only instrumentation for most of the track being Gray's dominant bass, Sensible's choppy chorused guitar and Scabies' booming, reverb-soaked kick and snare patterns. While much of the album harks back to earlier rock and pop eras, 'Twisted Nerve' sounds contemporary; its stripped-back monochromatic approach very much in step with Joy Division and The Cure's dark post-punk sound.

Each verse begins slowly with Vanian's serpentine vocal melody enhancing the lyric's sense of mystery. As the chorus approaches, the pace quickens, reflecting the narrator's racing pulse as danger nears: 'Go to the window and what do I see / The killer's face looking at me.' After the second such crescendo – where it is revealed that the killer tormenting our narrator is none other than (spoiler alert) himself, the arrangement becomes fuller and more expansive, with Ray Martinez' trumpet taking up the melody, tasteful piano and Sensible's stabbing guitar chords underpinning, a long delay echoing rhythmically across the track. Like 'These Hands' before it, 'Twisted Nerve' ably demonstrates Vanian's ability to channel his fascination with the moodier, more grisly aspects of film and popular culture into beautifully-realised dark pop vignettes: an ability which would set the tone not only for this LP but for much of the band's career.

'Hit Or Miss' (David Vanian / Paul Gray / Rat Scabies / Captain Sensible)

Paul Gray's first Damned songwriting contribution is another all-out rocker, harking back to the raw punk of the band's debut. Like the stylistically similar 'Drinking About My Baby', it predates the *Black Album* sessions, having originally been recorded by Gray's former band, Eddie and the Hot Rods. That version had a Rolling Stones-like mid-tempo swagger and a slightly punk attitude that couldn't conceal the band's pub rock roots. In contrast, The Damned really put the pedal to the metal, kept the basic structure intact and dramatically cranked the tempo and volume. Rat hammers the song along with his four-to-the-bar kick drum, while Gray's roving, melodic bass acts as a lead instrument over Sensible's tight, punchy rhythm guitars. The Captain also takes a couple of solos: the first in the timeless Chuck Berry mould; the second, a wild Hendrix-indebted concoction of screaming feedback and vibrato bar dive-bombs. Vanian leers and snarls his way through the tale of romantic misadventure, delivering with particular relish the New York Dolls-referencing payoff line, 'And I was looking for a kissss-ah!'.

The words don't amount to a great deal, and there's not much of a tune, but that barely matters – it's two and a half minutes of captivatingly exuberant rock 'n' roll from a great band at the peak of their powers. Like 'Drinking About My Baby', it does slightly break with the album's prevailing atmosphere, but it benefits from its end-of-side-one position, allowing the vinyl listener to reset somewhat before the next song.

'Dr Jekyll And Mr Hyde' (David Vanian / Paul Gray / Rat Scabies / Captain Sensible / Giovanni Dadamo)

The first side two song, finds the band back in mysterious, brooding form, opening with a delicate E minor acoustic guitar passage, Sensible playing a descending chord sequence against a ringing open B string, creating a series of eerie suspensions. The sequence repeats, with added bass and an electric guitar with a tremolo effect, heightening the sense of shadowy intrigue. When the full band kicks in, it sounds similar to 'Silly Kid's Games', with acoustic rhythm guitar, warm Hammond organ, and not a crashing power chord to be heard. The guitar and organ swap back and forth from E to D, Sensible adding chiming suspended-9th chords on an electric twelve-string, while Gray's lively bass keeps a solid E pedal note going underneath, rising to A and B at the end of each phrase.

Meanwhile, Vanian is in full late-night crooner mode, the seductive melody making excellent use of his rich lower register, as he – playing the role of Jekyll to a tee – tells of his nefarious alter-ego: 'I try to be true, he tries to be cruel / I'll hold you gently, but he'll smother you.' It's the perfect vehicle for Vanian's developing persona; and the smooth, stately backing, an ideal setting for his velvet tones. The song was co-written with Giovanni Dadamo, who had also co-written 'I Just Can't Be Happy Today' and who seemed to have an instinctive grasp of where the band – and their lead singer in particular – were heading thematically.

The middle section ramps up the theatricality, the band slipping unexpectedly into 5/4 time (an unusual thing for a punk group, especially before The Stranglers huge and rhythmically ambitious hit, 'Golden Brown' (1981)). Vanian breaks into a dramatic monologue, further elucidating the nature of his duality: 'Me, I'm on the side of the angels, but the devil's my best friend ... Two for the price of ... one?' It's completely over the top and utterly corny, but also great fun. Like all theatre, some suspension of disbelief is required, but Vanian really comes into his own here: a rock 'n' roll Christopher Lee, luring the listener in with svelte-but-deadly charm.

'Sick Of This And That' (David Vanian / Paul Gray / Rat Scabies / Captain Sensible)

This breezy blast of frenetic power-pop instantly sweeps the spooky cobwebs away. Composed by Rat, an early version was recorded under the title 'Whitecats', and the song does certainly seem to owe something to the hard-edged tunefulness of Scabies' erstwhile project. At a mere 1:47, it's the album's shortest song and eschews the more elaborate arrangements heard elsewhere, using just a core of guitar, bass and drums. The song takes off in frantic 2/4 time, Rat delivering an especially explosive performance, showing no sign of the one-handedness which allegedly hampered him during these sessions. Gray and Sensible bash out an upbeat verse chord sequence of E,/G#m/A and B (the same I, II, IV, V sequence that later underpinned The Housemartins' 1986 hit,

'Happy Hour'), and Vanian's vocal is equally chirpy, on a catchy tune, straight out of the 1950s pop playbook. Given the music's overwhelmingly positive feel, it's perhaps surprising that the lyrics are so utterly negative, expressing dissatisfaction with the world in a way that – even in 1980 – must have already seemed like a punk cliché: 'Sick of the government, sick of the police / Sick of the boredom, I want release.' Still, if we don't focus on the somewhat half-baked lyrics too much, this is pop-punk par excellence and acts as a handy palate cleanser before the epic drama to follow.

'The History Of The World (Part 1)' (David Vanian / Paul Gray / Rat Scabies / Captain Sensible)

Epic drama is no overstatement! This oblique view of the descent of man is almost operatic in its scope and bombastic dynamism. Having heard the band's earlier, Wessex Studios-recorded version, Chiswick's Roger Armstrong thought he smelled a hit. Eager to repeat the success of the *Machine Gun Etiquette* singles, he brought in Hans Zimmer to add synths (LOTS of synths!) and a chart-friendly production gloss to the Rockfield version.

The resulting recording is totally unlike anything the band had done before. It's swathed in layers of electronic sound, chiming synthetic pianos (not unlike those heard on Abba's 1975 mega-hit 'Mamma Mia', as Vanian has been known to note in live performance), swirling chordal pads, sweeping sound effects, choral vocals, with Rat's timpani-like tom rolls adding to the Wagnerian *sturm und drang*: at times almost reminiscent of the work of Jim Steinman, the famed songwriter/producer responsible for such gloriously-overblown hits as Meat Loaf's 'Bat Out Of Hell' (1977) and Bonnie Tyler's 'Total Eclipse Of The Heart' (1983). To make room for such big production, The Damned's performances are remarkably reined-in, with Rat's drums sounding almost clinical, Gray's bass keeping largely to solid on-the-beat root notes; Sensible's main contribution being some tasteful Hammond organ chords, his guitar making its presence felt only during the song's closing minute.

The title boldly proclaims the song to be 'the history of the world', and in a way, it is, but it's far from an exercise in linear storytelling. Instead, through imagery and allusion, we see humans supplanting the dinosaurs and hints of mankind's achievements and failures: the moon landing, the creation of music and literature, corruption, decadence and war. Along the way, Sensible (the song's principal author, although Scabies maintains that pop songwriter, BA Robertson, was the uncredited main melody writer) manages to drop in a typically odd selection of pop culture references. These include Adam Chance – a character from the then-popular soap, *Crossroads* – masked swashbuckler, Zorro, and Corporal Clott: a bungling soldier from *The Dandy* comic, here used as a metaphor for military incompetence leading to a world-ending event. 'No one alive and no one left / Nobody cares, or ain't you heard? / Looks like I'll take my dying breath / In the history of the world.' The

Cold War shadow looms large over the song, imparting a bitter fatalism that remains slightly chilling in spite of the track's larger-than-life pomposity.

Ultimately, it's an astonishing listen, with enigmatic lyrics that match the accompaniment, which blends psychedelia, prog and electropop elements into something that somehow still sounds like The Damned, even though it could hardly be further from the Stooges-inspired style of the Brian James era only three years earlier. As a single, it was perhaps too odd and ambitious for mass appeal, stalling at number 51 in the charts, with *Smash Hits* derisively comparing it to Supertramp. But make no mistake – this wonderfully over-the-top record is quintessential Damned.

'13th Floor Vendetta' (David Vanian / Paul Gray / Rat Scabies / Captain Sensible)

While much of *The Black Album* flirts with psychedelia, it's not until '13th Floor Vendetta' that things get really trippy. Much of the song is based around a simple repeating two-chord F#/F pattern: a semitone shift giving a smouldering flamenco-like feel, further emphasised through Sensible's nylon-strung acoustic guitar, throughout. Over a lithe, yet unobtrusive drums, bass and organ backing, the band present a veritable tone poem of massively reverb-drenched piano, backwards electric guitars, tape effects and angelic voices, taking full advantage of the stereo spectrum and using the studio almost as an instrument in itself. Vanian gives a powerful and nuanced performance, full-voiced on the cascading, flamenco-inspired opening verse melody, dropping to a gentle murmur for the two-line repeated phrase which is as close as this unusual song comes to a chorus, also channelling his inner Vincent Price for the spoken word section. The lyrics quote from Price's cult classic, *The Abominable Doctor Phibes* (1971): an endearingly oddball tale of an insane organist's quest for revenge against those he holds responsible for his wife's death. But Vanian turns this potentially corny subject matter into something quite enigmatic and enchanting. Suddenly at around the 3:40 mark, a final ominous backwards chord gives way to a solo piano playing a gentle, wistful G major theme, completely at odds with the tracks dominant sleek menace. A tasteful acoustic guitar chimes in, and this fascinating experiment ends on an unexpectedly pastoral note.

'Therapy' (David Vanian / Paul Gray / Rat Scabies / Captain Sensible / Fay Hart)

A series of booming tom-tom flurries introduce this track, guitar and bass joining in a haphazard fashion, before all lock into an unusual (for The Damned) strutting mid-tempo hard rock groove. Gray and Scabies hammer out a rock-solid rhythm in E, handclaps bolstering the stomping beat, while Sensible's twin-guitar tracks harmonise in 3rds on an obtuse, discordant melody. The intro section concludes in a major key with percussive fireworks, and Gray launches the song proper, with a commanding bass riff very much in the Lemmy-inspired 'Love Song' mould. Like that song, the ensuing track blends raging punk with melody to powerful effect, but 'Therapy' is a significantly darker, weirder prospect, with much less regard for commerciality or conventional pop song structure. Granted, we begin with a fairly straightforward verse and chorus, the verse following the bass intro chords, the chorus using the highly unusual sequence of G#/E/A/D#. This pattern repeats twice before giving way to what we assume is a middle eight – a call-and-response section, with Vanian's arch baritone responding to Sensible's yelled backing vocal questions. At this point, we might reasonably expect a third verse or chorus repeat, but instead, we get another section – Vanian now crooning over a jangling A major guitar figure, with a somewhat 'Dear Prudence'-like descending bass beneath the chord's ringing notes. But instead of circling back to any earlier section, there follows several minutes of instrumental, as the track disintegrates into psychedelic chaos, culminating in the Captain's avant-garde guitar-mangling, shrieks of feedback snaking across the stereo spectrum.

The lyrics – written with some assistance from Fay Hart: a UK-born LA scenester known at the time as Farrah Fawcett Minor – are something of an enigma. On the one hand, they question the validity of therapy, painting patients as 'Clones with Barclaycards', and therapists as 'Dirty men with their dirty looks'. On the other hand, by the end of the call and response bridge, our narrator seems to acknowledge his own need for therapy, albeit that of a different kind: 'Who needs therapy all night long? I do'. Finally, we, the listeners find ourselves in the position of therapist, getting a glimpse into the narrator's subconscious: 'I dream of pavements / Pavements cold and grey.' What does it all mean? Well, I'm no therapist.

It's an intriguing track, and framing the song's main body (which really only lasts for around 90 seconds) with four and a half minutes of instrumental, creates the impression that the song itself is a dream – emerging from and then receding back into, the subconscious.

'Curtain Call' (David Vanian / Paul Gray / Rat Scabies / Captain Sensible)

And so, we arrive at *The Black Album*'s crowning glory and the reason for its double-album status, taking up as it does, an entire vinyl side. Dave Vanian's songwriting talent had emerged surprisingly fully-formed on *Machine Gun Etiquette* after an inauspicious debut with the unremarkable 'Your Eyes' back in 1977. But nothing could've prepared the band or their fans for 'Curtain Call'. It was initially demoed at Wessex studios, under the rather less evocative title, 'Dave's Song'. In the *Black Album* expanded reissue booklet, Vanian recalled it 'started off as a three or four-minute song on my squeaky old harmonium in my dark, damp flat in Islington'. Over the course of a year, as the rest of the band offered suggestions, the song's scope and length grew massive; the band experimenting in the studio as never before, resulting in a widescreen epic, almost eighteen minutes long.

Over the sound of waves and birdsong, we begin at a stately pace, with the harmonium playing a droning A over a descending bass figure as Vanian sets the scene: 'The heat of the lights, the crack of the whip'. The lyrics are a beguiling riddle, rich in mysterious imagery, acting as both a meditation on performance from curtain-up to curtain call and a metaphysical musing on existence and death. We're a long way from 'Neat Neat Neat' here!

The track gradually gathers momentum, Gray adding pulsing bass, and Sensible providing some gentle reverberating clean-toned guitar touches as the vocal melody spirals and soars. The chords – A to Dm/A and F to G/F – are simple enough, yet far removed from the standard rock and pop patterns which informed much of the band's earlier work, and indeed the punk oeuvre in general. The track keeps building, a rumbling toms stampede heralding a powerful rhythm section. But just as we're settling into what appears as a more 'standard' Damned song, the drums fade away, and the piano and organ lead into another section. Over a lushly-melancholy piano accompaniment, Vanian softly intones a wistful melody (apparently written by Sensible) as the lyrics take on a weary, defeated tone: 'No more will I roam / Our childish dreams are soon outgrown ... Curtain call, about to fall.'

Most bands would see the seven-minute mark as the natural point to conclude such an epic. But for The Damned, this point was merely the launching pad for a voyage into the unknown. The piano fades, leaving only an ominously-sustained low organ chord, which serves as a convenient edit point where the track's two separate performances are spliced together.

We're in spacey, ambient territory now, with snatches of melody, eerie sound effects, and a dramatic violin passage (a tape loop taken from a recording of Rimsky-Korsakov's *Sheherazade*) drifting through our consciousness, the organ drone underpinning all. When the organ finally fades, a round of applause breaks out over the sound of footsteps: perhaps our narrator returning for his titular curtain call. A sharp burst of synthesizer suddenly interrupts the ambient sounds. Now a pulsing bass synth in A re-establishes key and rhythm. Organ, bass and drums gradually rejoin, and finally, Sensible takes a brief but excellent lead guitar solo. We now hear a reprise of the main 'verse' ('We're coming up from the deep / The lizard sheds its skin'), and it really does feel like we've re-emerged from some uncharted depths into the light. Finally, the band play the theme once more in full rock mode, Sensible's power chords let loose, with added slide guitar (not heard on a Damned record since 1977's 'One Way Love') and vigorous acoustic rhythm. As this triumphant encore fades, only the modulating synth throb remains. It's been a heck of a journey!

'Curtain Call' is a staggering achievement – a massive gamble that really shouldn't work but which succeeds spectacularly. It carries all the major elements of The Damned's sonic signature yet contains passages that could just as easily have been recorded by early Genesis, Pink Floyd or even Brian Eno. An array of audible influences extends far beyond the normal punk purview: from the dark organ-led psychedelia of The Doors and Brian Auger and the

Trinity to the motoric electronica of Kraftwerk, film soundtracks and a number of 19th and 20th-century classical composers who had recently piqued The Damned's interest. 'Curtain Call' broke every punk rule, but then again, The Damned had never cared much for rules.

'Love Song (Live)' (David Vanian / Algy Ward / Rat Scabies / Captain Sensible)

The live tracks commence with some disorganised faffing, as Rat thumps his kick drum and Sensible clangs around on guitar before Gray decides it's time to get going, launching into the familiar intro with almost as much venom as Algy Ward brought to the studio recording. The ensuing performance is tight and energetic, showcasing how quickly the band with Gray had cohered as a unit. It follows the studio version pretty closely, with only Vanian departing from the original template by singing a higher chorus vocal line; it can sometimes be difficult to project low notes with enough power to cut through a loud band, particularly one as raucous as The Damned! Throughout these live tracks, Sensible uses a chorus (artificial doubling) effect on his guitar. This was a popular trick to thicken the sound of single-guitar punk bands in the 1980s but has since fallen out of fashion, which slightly time-stamps these otherwise timeless performances.

'Second Time Around (Live)' (David Vanian / Algy Ward / Rat Scabies / Captain Sensible)

Here we have the *Machine Gun Etiquette* title track, albeit introduced with its original title from the White Cats days. Although taken at a furious pace, it's not quite as frenetic as the studio recording, and Vanian sings much of it in a lower register, which is certainly a good plan for avoiding losing one's voice early in the set, but which slightly dilutes the intensity. Still, it's a pretty great performance, notable for Paul Gray's spectacular bass work in the instrumental section.

'Smash It Up Parts 1 & 2 (Live)' (David Vanian / Algy Ward / Rat Scabies / Captain Sensible)

Part 1 is here faithful to the studio recording; perhaps a little faster and without the layer of studio gloss, but essentially the same. However, as Vanian introduces Part 2 with a cry of 'Smash it up!', we're immediately plunged into punkier waters, with the accelerated pace and Sensible's overdriven guitar providing a raw urgency not heard in the pristine power pop of the studio recording. Unusually, virtuoso bassist, Paul Gray, drops a noticeable clanger after the second chorus, on the way to the E minor breakdown, wandering hopelessly off-key for a couple of bars. There's also a duck call that crops up a few times during the last minute or so, sounding like a squeaky pet toy or a creaking door hinge! It's a testament to the chaotic, anything goes Damned spirit that these recordings are presented exactly as they happened, resisting the urge to sneakily retouch tracks afterwards, as was the practice on some live albums of the era.

'New Rose (Live)' (Brian James)

The band were clearly keen to use these live tracks as a showcase for their post-reunion material, and as a result, all but one of the songs chosen were originally from *Machine Gun Etiquette*. The sole exception is this rendition of the debut single, taken at a fiendish pace, lasting a mere 1:49. It's so fast that Rat has to significantly simplify his drum part, giving the record a Ramones-like linear drive that the slower but more explosive studio recording doesn't possess. It's exciting and certainly shows the reconstituted band could handle the Brian James-era material with ease – although there is a slight sense that they're zipping through the 'oldie' as quickly as possible so they can get back to what they really want to play.

'I Just Can't Be Happy Today (Live)' (David Vanian / Algy Ward / Rat Scabies / Captain Sensible / Giovanni Dadamo)

Here we find Sensible relinquishing guitar duties to play the signature organ part. There's a great, freewheeling energy to this performance, emphasising aggression over the original's cool mood. If there's anything to criticise, it's that the arrangement feels rather empty. On the studio recording, Sensible overdubbed guitar and a second organ part, playing chords beneath the melodic lines (His playing at the time was not advanced enough to combine chordal and melodic functions: footage of the band's shambolic *Old Grey Whistle Test* appearance shows the Captain playing this with just two fingers!). Minus these layers, Paul Gray is left with a lot of space to fill. His bass does sound huge, but overall, the track still sounds slightly incomplete.

'Plan 9 Channel 7 (Live)' (David Vanian / Algy Ward / Rat Scabies / Captain Sensible)

The Captain is back on guitar here, while another mysterious, uncredited character has taken over on organ (why they couldn't have done the same on the previous track is anybody's guess). Anyway, this is a great version of one of the band's finest songs. The original's sense of mystique is somewhat dialled-back in favour of more energy and raw power, with some terrific playing all round, the odd bum note notwithstanding. No one attempts the 'Come and join me' backing vocals, which is a shame, but Vanian is in fine voice, fearlessly tackling the falsetto outro without a second thought; and Sensible's guitar slashes, growls and soars heroically, nicely rounding off this live postscript to a spectacular album.

Strawberries (1982)

Personnel:
Rat Scabies: drums
Dave Vanian: vocals
Captain Sensible: guitars, keyboards, sitar, lead vocals on 'Life Goes On' and 'Don't Bother Me'
Paul Gray: Bass
Roman Jugg: keyboard solos
Additional personnel:
Simon Lloyd: brass on 'Generals'
Rachael Bor: cello on 'Pleasure and the Pain'
Recorded at Rockfield Studios
Record label: Bronze
Released: October 1982
Producer: The Damned and Hugh Jones
Highest chart position: UK: 15
Length: 48:12
Current edition: 2015 remastered reissue on Sanctuary Records.

The Damned were hard to place in the 1982 musical landscape. Punk – contrary to the widely accepted myth propagated by countless retrospectives – had not died with the Sex Pistols in 1978 and was actually healthy. It had, however, evolved (or devolved?) in a number of different directions. UK punk now fell into three distinct categories, albeit with some blurred edges. From seeds Crass planted, blossomed anarcho-punk: with bands like Subhumans, Poison Girls and Rudimentary Peni playing music often wildly creative, generally challenging, and always politically radical; Oi! grew in parallel with the skinhead movement renaissance – disciples of Sham 69 and Cock Sparrer playing meaty street-level punk with terrace chant-inspired vocals; and the UK hardcore scene (latterly known as UK82) focused on broadly-political sloganeering lyrics from spikey-topped urchins such as GBH and The Exploited, barked aggressively over bludgeoning Motorhead-inspired rhythms.

The emerging scene on the artier side of the punk diaspora would come to be known as gothic rock (the music press then misleadingly labelling it 'positive punk'), led by the likes of UK Decay and Bauhaus; while post-punk indie groups like Echo & the Bunnymen and The Teardrop Explodes successfully fused punk's energy with brooding psychedelia. The Damned could take credit for inspiring all these strands to a greater or lesser extent and yet didn't belong to any of them, having become seemingly too goth for the punks, too pop for the goths, and too punk for the pop fans.

Furthermore, though *The Black Album* had been a creative high watermark, this had not translated to sustained commercial success. The album sold respectably, but a single taken from the sessions – 'There Ain't No Sanity Clause' b/w 'Looking at You' from the Shepperton concert from which album side four was compiled – failed to make a dent in the festive chart: a shame, as the A-side slice of effortlessly-melodic and very silly Xmas cheer delivered at a blistering pace, is surely (along with the Ramones' 'Merry Christmas (I Don't Want To Fight Tonight)') one of the finest festive punk songs ever committed to vinyl.

As relations with Chiswick Records soured, 1981 saw the NEMS Records release of the excellent *Friday The 13th* EP, showcasing four tracks of power-pop-punk, continuing much in the mode of *The Black Album*'s more upbeat moments: 'Disco Man' is driving and anthemic, while 'The Limit Club' is moodier, bringing keyboards and Vanian's Scott Walker fixation, to the fore. 'Billy Bad Breaks' is hugely catchy, driven by some vigorous acoustic guitar and Paul Gray's finest bass line to date. A fine cover of The Rolling Stones' under-appreciated gem, 'Citadel', rounds the record off. The EP crept to number 50 in the UK but couldn't match the successful run of *Machine Gun Etiquette* singles, and as NEMS hit the financial skids, The Damned were left without a label.

Further complicating matters, Sensible had embarked on a solo career. Following 1981's excellent *This Is Your Captain Speaking* EP on Crass records, demos of the Captain's whimsical, gently psychedelic songs – deemed unsuitable for The Damned – found their way to A&M records, who signed him as a solo artist, leaving him in a considerably better position than the band that was still, theoretically, his main focus. The icing on the cake was the label releasing Sensible's recording of the evergreen *South Pacific* show tune, 'Happy Talk', which went all the way to number 1, suddenly making him a household name.

In the midst of all this, and now signed to yet another label: Bronze – home at the time to their old pals, Motorhead – The Damned went back into Rockfield to commence work on *Strawberries*. Keyboard player Roman Jugg – a former member of Welsh punks, Victimise – now augmented the *Black Album* line-up, drafted in to play the keyboards that were an increasingly integral part of The Damned's sound. Once again, the band chose to produce themselves, with Rockfield's in-house engineer, Hugh Jones, contributing enough to seven of the eleven tracks, to be credited as co-producer; and in the interests of ensuring that royalties were distributed evenly, all songs were again credited to the full band – although, after Paul Gray's acrimonious departure, these were amended: his credits separated out on some subsequent reissues.

The album title referred to a band saying: increasingly disillusioned with their audience, the band felt that playing their more sophisticated new material to hordes of braying, gobbing punks was 'Like feeding strawberries to pigs'. In the interests of not alienating their record-buying public, the full saying was not used. But the rear cover photo – showing a piglet staring blankly at the camera, surrounded by splattered fruit – amply illustrated the concept for those in the know.

While the album was in progress, Bronze issued 'Lovely Money' – recorded earlier that year – as a single. This drum-machine-powered satirical oddity featuring The Bonzo Dog Band's Viv Stanshall delivering a monologue was great fun but hardly representative of The Damned's new direction, although the blazing pop-punk of B-side 'I Think I'm Wonderful' was pleasingly reminiscent of *Machine Gun Etiquette*. The single outperformed the band's last few efforts, reaching number 42 in the UK: an unspectacular but respectable showing.

After *The Black Album*'s glorious excesses, *Strawberries* is compact and focussed, with any experimental tendencies confined within the bounds of tightly arranged songs. Nevertheless, it's still broad in scope, encompassing more musical styles and a wider instrumental palette than ever before. It's also, for the most part, simply great pop music and deservedly climbed to number 15: the band's highest placing to date. However, to some extent *Strawberries* also represents a group pulling in different directions, and the personal/musical tensions that had always made The Damned such a vital and fascinating listening experience had boiled over into studio fisticuffs, with the ever-volatile Rat taking umbrage at Gray's lyrics for 'Pleasure And The Pain', and expressing his feelings with his fists. They managed to patch things up to complete the album, but Gray departed in March 1983, to join veteran hard-rockers UFO. By the time the album-buying public heard from The Damned again, they would be a very different band.

'Ignite' (Dave Vanian / Captain Sensible / Rat Scabies)

The album begins with this fierce statement of intent – an anthemic headlong gallop showing the band could easily keep pace with the UK82 crowd and write catchier songs into the bargain. There's nothing sophisticated going on here: the song's driving guitar riff is little more than a simple B and G vamp; the lyrics, for all their intent to 'set the world alight', are merely about getting fired up for a big night out; and the catchy refrain abandons words altogether, in favour of that punk staple of massed voices singing 'woah!'. The song seems specifically designed to generate excitement at the start of a live set; get the audience on their feet, adrenaline pumping, singing along without needing to know the words. It has served exactly that purpose at many a Damned gig, working the same way as an album opener.

Nevertheless, there's more going on here than mere brainless thrash. Unlike much of the more 'hardcore' punk of the era, there's real melodic content here, Vanian singing with great conviction. Indeed, the usually slightly cool and detached singer really lets rip, with some wonderfully over-the-top ad-libs – ' I wanna see you burn!'. 4:52 is also considerably longer than your average punk rock song, allowing room for dynamic peaks and valleys and plenty of suitably incendiary Hendrix-inspired Sensible wah-wah leads. Finally, the whole thing collapses into a maelstrom of feedback and Vanian's hysterical cry of 'I'm on fire baby!'. Overall, 'Ignite' is a terrific start, forcefully restating The Damned's punk credentials without sacrificing their newfound musicality and sense of drama.

'Generals' (Paul Gray)

Paul Gray's first song contribution here is tremendous: Cold War paranoia filtered through an immaculately crafted cinematic power-pop protest song. Inspired by a visit to the divided Berlin's stark contrast between the decadent, capitalist West and the austere, authoritarian East, Gray paints a startling, apocalyptic vision of the potential consequences of tension escalation, with ordinary people on both sides paying the price, while those in command, seemingly escape: 'And only the wounded remain / The generals have all left the game / With no will to fight, they'll fade with the light / There's nobody left they can blame.' However, in the final verse, it seems that even the generals may not escape the carnage, in which there are 'No leaders anymore, in the bunker dead', eventually concluding that 'The whole world is going insane', as Rat's martial snare drum fades into the distance.

Insistent electric piano drives the moody, minor-key verses, Gray's full-toned roving bass line underpinning, creating a sound similar to The Stranglers' 'No More Heroes' (1977). Guitars are used sparingly, adding colour rather than providing a focal point, with a twanging James-Bond-theme-style line under the verse's second half (An effective musical shorthand for Cold War intrigue), and high 'morse code' octaves in the chorus, recalling the guitar hook from The Supremes' 'You Keep Me Hangin' On' (1966). The chorus itself is built on a rich, almost classical chord progression apparently co-opted from Swedish hit machine Abba.

As with Vanian's harmonium compositions, writing on keyboard steered Gray away from the more obvious sequences that naturally fall under a guitarists' fingers; using suspended and inverted chords to create and resolve tension with a skill one might not expect from the bassist of a punk band. The instrumental section drops into a doom-laden E minor with a half-time feel, as Simon Lloyd's two horn tracks vie for space: a squall of jazz-like sax representing the *laissez-faire* West, and a seeming bugle call signifying the militaristic East, eventually coalescing in a single line as the song enters its climactic double chorus.

Released as a single in November 1982 – backed with the glistening harpsichord pop of 'Disguise' and the gnarly psych-punk oddity, 'Citadel Zombies' – 'Generals' deserved to be a huge hit. But, due to the financially failing Bronze Records' poor promotion, it sadly failed to chart. Still, it's a wonderful song, showing the band could still expand their horizons within the three-minute pop format and highlighting what an asset Gray was as a songwriter.

'Stranger On The Town' (Dave Vanian / Captain Sensible / Rat Scabies)

Three dramatic chords accompany Rat's cacophonous drum fills and squealing horns, presumably played by The Members and Icehouse musician Simon Lloyd, who is only credited for 'Generals', but remains very much in evidence here. From the silence that follows, Gray establishes a driving bass line, doubled on piano to the left and Hammond B3 to the right. After drums and cowbell, then horns and guitar (playing more of those Supremes-inspired high octaves) join in, the band locks into an unmistakable Motown/Northern soul groove: unusual for a band with a reputation largely built on obnoxious white-boy rock, and further evidence of their increasing refusal to be pigeonholed. The retro-soul sound was in vogue in the UK at the time, with revivalists like Dexy's Midnight Runners and punkish mods such as The Jam and Secret Affair, all tipping their hats to classic Stax and Motown, so it was a good time for The Damned to acknowledge their fondness for that strain of vintage R&B.

With lyrics bemoaning the loneliness and unfairness of being ostracised in unfamiliar surroundings, it's a catchy piece of melodic soul/pop. The standard Motown ingredients are in place, but Rat's drums – which move effortlessly between slick soul stomp and flailing Keith Moon-like rock fills – circumvent out-and-out pastiche. Sensible's crunching guitar, too, really makes its presence felt from around the two-minute mark. The verse/chorus/bridge format proceeds as expected, and we might assume the song is ready to wrap up by around 3:30. Instead, a tense sequence of chromatic rising chords mirrors our narrator's growing anxiety: 'Even in a crowd you're all alone / It's so far from home / There's faces all around ... You gotta get away.' This leads unexpectedly to a triumphant new section, almost serving as an alternative chorus, with Vanian ascending to his upper register, the horns blasting out C major chords while Gray holds down a dramatic low G pedal note. There are some great vocal harmonies, new boy Jugg gets a chance to shine on the Hammond organ, and there's a general feeling of the track lifting up a notch before finally fading out.

'Dozen Girls' (Dave Vanian / Captain Sensible / Rat Scabies / Billy Karloff)

After an enigmatic keyboard arpeggio echoes its way across the stereo spectrum, Vanian's cry of 'Alright!' introduces a mean, Stones-like guitar riff before Scabies' thudding floor toms bring in the full band. A relentless snare-on-every-beat stomp – reminiscent of The Kinks' 'David Watts' (1967) and The Undertones' 'My Perfect Cousin' (1980) – drives the track along. Lyrically, the song has a similar premise to the above-mentioned songs, as our envious narrator bemoans his unnamed antagonist's success with the opposite sex; a neat shift from B to a wistful F#m in the chorus, underscoring his almost-poignant plea: 'Tell me why / I don't know why he's got a dozen girls.' The envious tone is mixed with a grudging admiration, conceding that 'He's got charm, he's got style', but gives way to mockery by the time we reach the outro, where Sensible leads the marvellously silly playground chant of 'He's alright and he don't care / He's got thermal underwear!' Interestingly, Billy Karloff (who also helped out on 'Wait For The Blackout') has a writing co-credit on some – but not all – versions of the album, so it's unclear exactly what his contribution here may have been.

The track is snappy, beautifully constructed pop-punk, with some great details, such as the introductory keyboard motif resurfacing as part of verse two's arrangement, nice chorus vocal harmonies, and Sensible's duelling lead tracks which eventually gel into Thin-Lizzy-style harmony lines. Jugg gets another good workout during the extended outro, and the four and a half minutes positively fly by.

'Dozen Girls' was released as a single in September 1982; in a slightly different version, with added horns and the 'thermal underwear ... ' hook replaced by a roll-call of girls names. Backed with the odd-but-fun Simmons-drums-powered punk of 'Take That'; the utterly stupid Casio keyboard ditty 'Mine's A Large One Landlord'; and Sensible's brief but powerful animal rights piano ballad, 'Torture Me', 'Dozen Girls' deserved to be a huge hit. But it failed to chart, proving once more that the record-buying public didn't know what was good for them!

'The Dog' (Dave Vanian / Captain Sensible / Rat Scabies)

Overall, *Strawberries* sees The Damned toning down their gothic tendencies and taking in a broad range of styles to create a multi-faceted pop record. However, this unsettling ballad from the quill of Dave Vanian is a deep dive into the sinister depths previously explored on the likes of 'These Hands' and '13th Floor Vendetta'. It paints a portrait of the character Claudia, from Anne Rice's hugely successful 1976 novel, *Interview With the Vampire*. Its depiction of vampires – not as mere fiends to be feared, but as complex, romantic and sexually magnetic figures – was very influential, not only on the horror genre but on the burgeoning goth movement. Vanian had a particular fascination with Claudia: a decades-old vampire, forever condemned to live in the body of a five-year-old – 'Like a swimmer in a secret sea / Undecayed for all eternity', as the lyric put it.

A foreboding horror-soundtrack-style introduction – bass piano notes tolling ominously over a dissonant keyboard arpeggio – leads us into a seductively lush piano ballad in D minor over a soft rumba played on congas. Vanian is in his finest lounge lizard mode, and the mellow backing and subtle Latin percussion almost steer the track into easy-listening territory, at least until the urgent staccato piano chords bring a sense of peril to the line 'Better stay away from Claudia'.

The track's inviting smoothness only serves to make its descent into disorder more disconcerting, as the rhythm gradually falls apart, the piano hits jarring chords, and Sensible adds clanging, hard-edged guitar stabs. Wordless vocals singing a stark open-5th interval, reverberate menacingly, and an up-close recording of a real snarling dog (which, eerily enough, apparently turned up outside the studio just as the backing track was being recorded), complete the chilling soundscape. It makes for one of the more genuinely unnerving and least campy of The Damned's ventures into the macabre, and is a great end to side one of the original LP.

Above: The moody, magnificent young Damned, ready to take on the world in 1976.

Left: The Damned hit the ground running with *New Rose*, the first ever UK punk single, and still one of the most exhilarating records ever released.

Left: The front cover of *Damned, Damned, Damned* perfectly capturing the slapstick anarchy of the band's early years. *(Stiff Records)*

Right: The Kandinsky-inspired design, created by Barney Bubbles for the Damned's troubled second LP, *Music For Pleasure*. *(Stiff Records)*

Above: The Damned live on stage, from the rear cover of their debut LP. Note Captain Sensible's face, pasted onto the side of a monitor speaker! *(Stiff Records)*

Below: A rare shot of the short-lived late-1977 line-up, featuring Jon Moss and Lu Edmonds. *(Erica Echenberg, Stiff Records)*

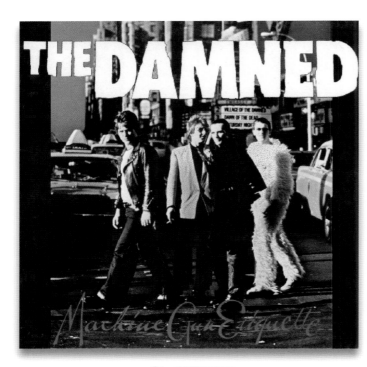

Left: The boys take to the streets of New York on the cover of their triumphant comeback album, *Machine Gun Etiquette. (Chiswick Records)*

Right: The Captain's cartoon alter-ego, 'Mr God Awful Ugly', guides us through the guitar chords to *Smash It Up* on the inner sleeve of *Machine Gun Etiquette. (Chiswick Records)*

Right: Rat Scabies, the percussive powerhouse behind many of The Damned's finest records, and one of punk's most distinctive stylists. *(Chiswick Records)*

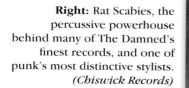

Left: The ever-suave Dave Vanian, whose vampiric style was a crucial catalyst for the early Goth movement. *(Chiswick Records)*

Right: Captain Sensible steps into the spotlight, performing 'Jet Boy Jet Girl', backed by The Softies on the B-side of the 1982 single of 'Wait For The Blackout', released to promote Big Beat's single-LP reissue of *The Black Album*. *(Big Beat Records)*

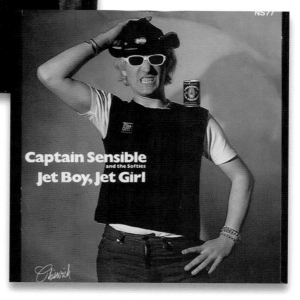

Captain Sensible
and the Softies
Jet Boy, Jet Girl

Left: *The Black Album*'s eerie cover art reflects the darker tone of this ambitious double album masterpiece. *(Chiswick Records)*

Right: The band, with new recruit Paul Gray (left) take a break in the rural surroundings of Rockfield Studios, during the recording of *The Black Album.* *(Chiswick Records)*

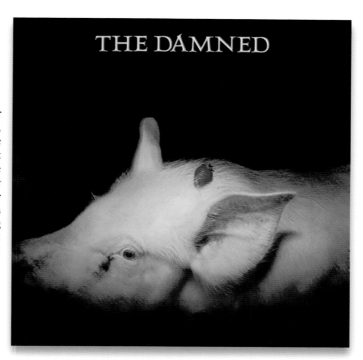

THE DAMNED

Right: The cover of *Strawberries*, referring to the band's view that playing their more sophisticated new music to their old punk fans was 'like feeding strawberries to pigs'! (*Bronze Records*)

The Damned

Phantasmagoria

Left: Model Susie Bick poses in a graveyard for the cover of *Phantasmagoria,* reflecting the darker, slicker and more serious image of the new-look major label Damned. *(MCA Records)*

Left: The Captain in traditional red beret and shades on the set of *The Young Ones*, one of his final appearances with The Damned before leaving to concentrate on his solo career. *(BBC)*

Right: A cobweb-strewn Dave Vanian really gets into the Halloween spirit on *The Young Ones* *(BBC)*

Left: An especially-spooky transitional Damned power through 'Nasty' on *The Young Ones,* with both Captain Sensible and Roman Jugg on guitar. *(BBC)*

Right: Dave Vanian in Goth-pop poster boy mode, promoting 'Eloise' on *Top Of The Pops*. *(BBC)*

Left: Roman Jugg, the Welsh *wunderkind* who emerged as the Damned's main creative force during the MCA years. *(BBC)*

Right: Bryn Merrick and a frock-coated Dave Vanian making a TV appearance on *Saturday Live* at the height of The Damned's mainstream success.

Above: The Damned's wonderfully-bombastic version of Barry Ryan's baroque-pop classic 'Eloise' would catapult them to new commercial heights, but also set the bar impossibly high for their subsequent releases. *(MCA Records)*

Above: No longer a gang of mis-matched oddballs, The Damned strike a unified image in this *Phantasmagoria*-era promo shot. *(MCA Records)*

Above: The bright, inviting cover of *Anything*, the band's somewhat creatively threadbare second album for MCA. *(MCA Records)*

Above: From Gothic dandies to rebel rockers: The Damned's new image for 1986 was heavy on the leather! *(MCA Records)*

Left: The US release of *Not of This Earth*, perhaps the most controversial album in the Damned's back catalogue. *(Cleopatra Records)*

Right: The UK release of *Not Of This Earth,* was retitled *I'm Alright Jack And The Bean Stalk* and packaged with a fancy lenticular cover design, but still contained the same confusingly un-Damned-like music! *(Marble Orchard Recordings)*

Right: The retro horror comic-style sleeve of *Grave Disorder*, a remarkable return to form for the rejuvenated band. *(Nitro Records)*

Left: The new-look 21st century version of The Damned posing in the photo shoot for *Grave Disorder*. *(Nitro Records)*

THE DAMNED

SO, WHO'S PARANOID?

Left: *So, Who's Paranoid?* continued The Damned's creative renaissance, although it failed to make a significant commercial impact. *(The English Channel)*

Left: Captain Sensible onstage and in his element, circa 2017. *(Spinefarm Records, Search And Destroy Records)*

Above: Rockfield revisited: The Damned recreate a classic pose in 2019, as they return to the fabled studio where they recorded *The Black Album* and *Strawberries*. *(Spinefarm Records, Search And Destroy Records)*

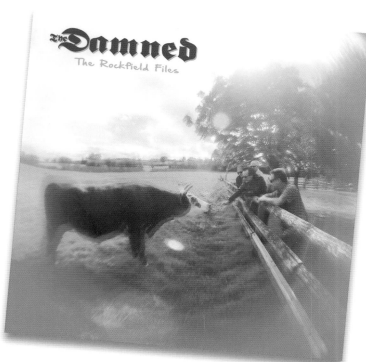

Left: *The Rockfield Files* continued the band's late-career resurgence with four excellent new tracks that sit comfortably alongside their best work. *(Spinefarm Records, Search And Destroy Records)*

Above: Well, I'll be Damned! The four original members bury the hatchet, with plans to play together again for the first time in thirty years. *(The Damned)*

'Gun Fury (Of Riot Forces)' (Dave Vanian / Captain Sensible / Rat Scabies)

Side two begins with this intriguing political punk/1960s folk rock/psychedelia blend. The lyrics, decrying authoritarian violence – as if from an early Clash or Stiff Little Fingers song – make a strong, simple statement against State aggression: 'They hate the public they defend / They call the shots from start to end ... Who dares resist the gun fury of riot forces?'

The music, however, is anything but simplistic agit-punk. Sure, Sensible's opening guitar riff has a punky snarl to it, but once the track settles into its swaying 5/4 groove, the immediate comparison that springs to mind is not The Clash, but Pentangle: Bert Jansch and John Renbourn's late-1960s folk-jazz troupe; specifically their song 'Light Flight' (1969). Both the chord sequence and the unusual rhythmic accents recall that track, with Rat's drums, in particular, sounding like a harder-hitting version of Terry Cox's gently-brushed pattern (Although Jansch and company confound their rhythm further, inserting a bar of two after every two bars of 5/4). Sensible plays jangling arpeggios throughout with an open G drone, overdubbing searing Indian-raga-inspired backwards lead breaks. Jugg's piano plays a tasteful countermelody, once again recalling David Greenfield's Stranglers work, and as the song draws to a close, some reversed percussion completes the trippy soundscape. Another successful Damned experiment, showing they could address political topics but avoid the generic trappings of 'political punk'.

'Pleasure and the Pain' (Paul Gray)

It was this surprisingly tender keyboard-driven love song that apparently caused the violent outburst that brought tensions between Rat and Paul Gray to a head, resulting in Gray's departure from the band. In Kieron Tyler's essential biography, *Smashing It Up: A Decade of Chaos with The Damned,* Scabies states: 'The lyrics, 'These feelings deep inside me' ... It was too personal for me and I didn't relate to it'. This lyric doesn't actually appear in the song, but even if it had, it's hard to see how it could upset Rat enough to punch anyone, and one suspects other issues may have been at the root of the dispute: Gray had recently suggested his girlfriend as the band's new manager, whereas Rat's preferred candidate was his own father, John Millar. To be fair to Rat, the lyrics really aren't amazing: a rather generic meditation on love's turmoil, with a bit of a sixth-form poetry feel, and one couplet that rhymes the word 'inside' with itself! Nevertheless, Vanian delivers them with a rare sincerity, to disarming effect.

The arrangement is sharp, snappy, and artfully orchestrated without succumbing to cloying mush. Bright piano chords and Gray's propulsive bass, dominate the mix, with organ and cello (played by Dolly Mixture's Rachael Bor) providing colour, and Sensible's tasteful, clean guitar adding a low-key hint of R&B. Furthermore, for all Scabies' reluctance, he gives a tight, powerful performance which serves the song beautifully. As Gray's songs go, 'Pleasure

And The Pain' may not be quite on par with the magnificent 'Generals', but – the odd dodgy lyric aside – it is an excellent piece of smart pop, with a level of taste and sophistication that would defy the band's critics.

'Life Goes On' (Dave Vanian / Captain Sensible / Rat Scabies)
The first of two songs on the album to feature Captain Sensible on lead vocals, this slice of melancholic, dreamy indie-pop marks another bold departure. It's founded on Gray's simple, distinctive bass riff, which proved to be so catchy it was virtually co-opted by Killing Joke a couple of years later, as the guitar riff for their hit, 'Eighties'; which in turn provided the basis for Nirvana's 1991 smash, 'Come As You Are'. However, in The Damned's hands, this motif is used as a launch pad for neither ominous post-punk nor grunge dynamics, instead underpinning an ethereal sound wash closer in style to the likes of Echo & the Bunnymen or even The Smiths. Buoyed by some sprightly-but-restrained drumming, delicate muted single-note guitar lines – soaked in chorus and reverb for a pretty, shimmering effect – sit above warm organ chord layers: a million miles from the overdriven rock 'n' roll heroics we've come to expect from the Captain – revealing once again his remarkable versatility.

Sensible's unaffected everyman vocal delivery is perfectly suited to the lyric's wistful, resigned tone – existential musings on our tendency to persevere, despite life's apparent futility: 'Life goes on and on and on/If you think it's all gone wrong, go on and on and on'. It moves to a major key for the refrain's deadpan instruction to 'Always remember, this is the happiest day of your life'. Only in the middle-eight is the mood of tranquil reflection interrupted, with a turbulent series of chord changes ramping up tension, as our narrator comes to the decision he must seize the day and take control of his life, rather than resign himself to fate: 'Life is for always / Take your time, who cares what fools say? / I don't mind, 'cos this is my day / I'll live it my way.' Having come to this revelation, we then settle back into the dreamy verse, now with subtle acoustic guitar arpeggios giving texture. A brief, tastefully melodic solo from Sensible rounds off this thoughtful and really quite beautiful track.

'Bad Time for Bonzo' (Dave Vanian / Captain Sensible / Rat Scabies)
1980s punk bands thrived on songs lampooning Ronald Reagan and Margaret Thatcher, the twin pillars of that decade's rampant right-wing populism. The Damned had once claimed to take an apolitical stance, but since Brian James' departure, their work gradually included more and more sociopolitical commentary, and now it was their turn to take a pot-shot at Reagan. In typical Damned style, the approach is playful rather than polemic, but no less effective for that. The title references Reagan's 1951 movie, *Bedtime for Bonzo*, in which the future president plays a psychologist experimentally raising a chimpanzee as a human child. As Reagan entered the political field, his detractors soon nicknamed him after the chimp, and The Damned carry on that tradition here, as did Ramones on their classic 'Bonzo Goes To Bitburg' (1985), which

addressed the president's controversial decision to pay his respects at the graves of Nazi soldiers. 'Bad Time For Bonzo' is more general in its critique, painting Reagan as a delusional ham; a second-rate actor selling the people a second-rate fantasy – 'Bonzo's always dreaming / He'd like you to be dreaming too' – and concluding that 'We'd best re-write the script while we can'.

This is set to some of the band's finest pop-punk to date. A hard-driving rock 'n' roll riff in A underpins the verses, with stabbing organ chords recalling The Sir Douglas Quintet's 1965 garage band classic, 'She's About a Mover'. This gives way to a wonderfully poppy chorus with gleaming harmonies and nifty overlapping call and response vocal lines. Initially in the key of G, the chorus is unexpectedly transposed down to E major for its final, extended iteration, where the expected key change norm would be to move up. Finally, the driving pace relents, the track concluding with a lullaby-like passage, Vanian crooning softly over gentle piano, ushering the listener into the dream the lyrics promise/threaten.

'Under the Floor Again' (Dave Vanian / Captain Sensible / Rat Scabies)

Based on the true story of Norman Green – a Wigan resident who, having been questioned by the police in connection with the death of an 87-year old woman, 'disappeared', hiding for eight years in his own home, concealed under the floorboards beneath his sofa. This is a majestic example of the dark, yearning psych-pop The Damned do so well. Over Sensible's shimmering tremolo guitar and a plaintive organ chord, Vanian mournfully croons: 'Under the floor again / Once I was up and in the air, but now I'm down.' It would be easy for a lyric to simply play up how outlandish the situation was; The Damned, on the other hand, manage to provide a disarming level of pathos while still acknowledging the inherent absurdity of our protagonist's predicament. Written as a first-person narrative, Vanian embodies the narrator with real empathy – the roguish voice that in 'Wait for the Blackout' made his basement's darkness sound so inviting, now suffocating in enforced sensory deprivation: 'Three feet of life is all I have, and rats to feed.'

A sitar in the mix emphasises the track's mid-to-late 1960s roots with echoes of the Stones' 'Paint It Black' (1966), and as the rhythm section kicks in, there's a distinctly psychedelic feel. Things get even trippier as Sensible's voice intrudes, singing in harmony with himself – 'So who was the girl we saw last night?' – in a brief section of off-kilter pop recalling Syd Barrett-era Pink Floyd. A disorienting long delay from left to right represents our narrator's confusion and panic as a curious child suddenly interrupts his self-imposed solitude. At around the 3:10 mark, the bass and drums drop out, a new section emerging in funereal half-time. The key of E minor and soft, wordless vocal harmonies cement the sorrowful mood, and as Rat's drums crash back in, we're in later Pink Floyd territory as Sensible launches into a soaring extended solo, reminiscent of Dave Gilmour's celebrated work on 'Comfortably Numb' (1979).

Ultimately, 'Under The Floor Again' is the work of an accomplished rock band, well versed in the vocabulary of numerous styles and confident enough to use the tools at their disposal with no perceived boundaries or regard for critical expectations.

'Don't Bother Me' (Dave Vanian / Captain Sensible / Rat Scabies)
After the dramatic 'Under The Floor Again', the album concludes with this curious novelty number, featuring the record's second Captain Sensible lead vocal and his last Damned album contribution for nearly twenty years. It's effectively a Sensible solo track, built on a loping, off-balance drum loop, with gradually building layers of organ and electric/acoustic guitars. It's reminiscent of some of The Kinks' slightly more whimsical, music-hall-inspired moments and certainly closer to the kind of material Sensible might issue on a solo record than The Damned's generally darker rock sound. The Captain reels off a comically misanthropic list of his personal gripes – including the nuclear industry, rock stars, women wearing furs, and Tony Hatch's *Crossroads* theme music – before an unequivocal conclusion of 'Go away ... Not interested!'

Showcasing the Captain as the ironic light-entertainment personality he had unwittingly become, 'Don't Bother Me' brings a little more levity to what has overall been a brighter-toned record than the preceding *Black Album*, but one that, sadly, represents a bittersweet farewell for Captain Sensible, who would be absent from the band's next few albums.

Phantasmagoria (1985)

Personnel:
Dave Vanian: Lead vocals
Roman Jugg: Guitar, keyboards, lead vocals on 'Edward The Bear', backing vocals
Bryn Merrick: Bass, backing vocals
Rat Scabies: Drums
Additional personnel:
Andy Richards: Keyboards
Paul Shepley: Keyboards
Gary Barnacle: Saxes and brass
Louis Jardim: Percussion
Steve Nieve: Keyboard inspiration on 'Sanctum Sanctorum'
Recorded at Eel Pie Recording Studios, London
Record label: MCA
Released: July 1985
Producer: Jon Kelly, except 'Grimly Fiendish' produced by Bob Sargeant and The Damned
Highest chart position: UK: 11
Length: 39:19
Current edition: 2009 double-CD expanded remastered reissue on Universal Records.

Given that *Strawberries* was an artistic triumph and had respectable commercial success, the band, by all rights, should've entered 1983 on a high. Instead, with Paul Gray's departure and Bronze Records financial collapse, The Damned found themselves in a sorry state, without a bassist or record label. The first problem at least was easily solved: Jugg simply recruiting his old Victimise bandmate, Bryn Merrick. But the promotional demands of Sensible's A&M solo deal left him with less and less time and energy for The Damned. While the Captain was busy with his other ventures, the remaining four members began playing gigs as Naz Nomad and the Nightmares, eschewing Damned songs in favour of classic psych and garage-band classics that had inspired them (A concept similar to The Dukes of Stratosphear – the psychedelic alter-ego of Swindon art-pop alchemists, XTC – who emerged the following year). This led to releasing a full album for Big Beat Records, titled, *Give Daddy the Knife Cindy* (1984): a collection of faithful reworkings of 1960s classics, which found the band taking on new pseudonyms (Roman was Sphinx Svenson, while Dave was, of course, Naz Nomad).

The Damned finally managed to reconvene, releasing on their own label the superb 'Thanks For The Night' single: an exciting blast of fierce-yet-melodic punk, the original version of which had appeared on Sensible's second solo LP, *The Power of Love* (1983). The B-side was the equally excellent 'Nasty': a fearsome rocker that Jugg (mostly) penned for the band's appearance on the anarchic sitcom, *The Young Ones*. The 12' single also included 'Do The Blitz': a fun tune, giving Vanian a chance to unleash his inner Gene Vincent. *The Young Ones* appearance marked something of a turning point for the band. As the episode had a Halloween theme, The Damned dressed accordingly. Vanian, of course was already in his gothic finery, which in recent years had only grown more flamboyant, but now the others – with the exception of Sensible – followed suit: teasing out their hair, donning frilly shirts and frock coats. In contrast, Sensible's sole concession was to borrow Jugg's coffin-shaped Vox Phantom guitar for the show. As a result – while The Damned had always been distinct individuals with their own styles and identities – Vanian, Jugg, Scabies and Merrick now looked like a cohesive unit, with Sensible the odd man out. The cracks were showing. By the end of August, Sensible had left the band.

With the Captain out of the picture, Jugg was free to move to guitar – his first instrument – a position he already occupied in Naz Nomad and the Nightmares. After the *Young Ones* taping, the band elected to keep their Gothic attire, presenting a unified, marketable image. Furthermore, minus Sensible's unpredictable, scene-stealing antics, their live show was tight and thoroughly professional, with Vanian very much the centre of attention.

Amazingly, The Damned were suddenly commercially viable, and in October, signed a deal with major US label, MCA. Their first MCA single – 'Grimly Fiendish', released in March 1985 – was promoted with a big budget (by Damned standards) music video and a multi-format release, rising to an impressive number 21 in the UK. The follow-up – 'Shadow Of Love' – did almost as well, peaking at number 25 in June. Then, in July, *Phantasmagoria* was released, reaching number 11, confirming beyond doubt that this new Damned was a commercial force to be reckoned with.

It was immediately clear that much had changed within the Damned camp. Rather than presenting different, sometimes conflicting, personalities and a kaleidoscopic array of influences, the focus was now firmly on Dave Vanian, the music and image forming an extension of his stage persona.

The album cover sets the tone: a moody black and white shot of model (and future wife of Nick Cave), Susie Bick, clad in a black cloak, standing before a dramatically lit cemetery. The band photos, rendered in antique-looking sepia, show them with teased-out gothic locks, looking serious and enigmatic while posing with twigs and branches: a far cry from the pie-throwing anarchy of yesteryear. This newfound seriousness carried over to the music too. Certainly, there were still hints of humour here and there, but the snarky satire and goofy fun that Sensible brought had largely been expunged in favour of a grandiose melodrama. Producer, Jon Kelly, brought a contemporary, chart-friendly sound, with layered synths and processed drum sounds, which, although cutting-edge at the time, now date the LP more than any of their earlier releases. To a Sensible-era fan, *Phantasmagoria* may sound a tad po-faced and sterile, but it can't be denied that it's a superbly crafted, tightly-focused slab of 1980s goth-pop-rock that undoubtedly earned The Damned many new fans. Plus, the band's highly enjoyable, totally overblown cover of Barry Ryan's 'Eloise' was a number 3 hit in 1986 (packaged with some later *Phantasmagoria* editions), representing a massive commercial peak for the band.

'Street of Dreams' (Rat Scabies / Dave Vanian / Roman Jugg / Bryn Merrick)

The album begins in a fashion very unlike The Damned: smoky tenor sax with a long delay and oodles of reverb, sounding very much the epitome of 1980s slickness. Saxophonist, Gary Barnacle, an accomplished session musician, had established solid punk credentials, recording with the likes of The Clash and the Ruts, but had more recently appeared on hits by Tina Turner, Kim Wilde and many others. Fortunately, as Rat kicks in with a steady toms rumble and Bryn's bass establishes a solid B root-note throb, the cocktail lounge soloing gives way to a soul-influenced horn section, playing unobtrusive but punchy riffs that complement the song nicely. Jugg's guitar is spare and carefully arranged, his brief lead fills and simple arpeggios made to sound huge with cavernous reverb: the overuse of which is one factor making the album sound rather 'of its time' now, along with the ubiquitous synth pads occupying every available gap in the mix.

For all the unnecessary production gloss, the song itself is strong, with a bold minor-key melody, perfectly suited to Vanian's baritone, and a catchy wordless chorus backing vocal hook. The lyrics, too, are effective, issuing a call-to-arms to outcasts and oddballs everywhere: 'The deadbeats and the dispossessed / The seekers of unlikeliness.' The song suggests they may struggle to fit the real world, but creativity and imagination unify them: 'We may be the haunted men / But we can hold our heads up when / We're walking down the street of dreams.' It's a fine sentiment and a great rallying cry for the many new fans the band were suddenly acquiring. The song is really only let down by a fussy, overlong arrangement which is too reliant on gimmickry. It rolls out every trick in the book, from layered harmony guitars and Latin percussion to cheesy synthesized faux-Spanish guitar and booming timpani. It's all very grand but doesn't really play to the band's strengths, with Scabies and Merrick, in particular, keeping things pared down, perhaps to leave room for all this nonsense. It's a great song, but it could sound even greater if shorn of around two minutes of time and about ten tracks of overdubs.

'Shadow of Love' (Dave Vanian / Rat Scabies / Roman Jugg / Bryn Merrick)

This second single from the album was a substantial hit, helped by a slick promo video featuring a tiny Damned performing in a doll's house under the watchful eye of a black-caped gothic maiden. It's a punchy, atmospheric pop song with a commanding Vanian vocal. The track rides on a prominent, catchy bass line and a distinctive, driving drum rhythm, creating a country two-step or rockabilly feel, especially when Rat slips into the chorus' snare shuffle. In fact, the whole song has something of a moody 1950s pop feel;

with a more organic backing, you could imagine Gene Vincent – or even a Sun-Records-era Elvis Presley – performing it. But the ever-present synth pads leave a thoroughly mid-1980s sonic fingerprint; not to mention Roman's guitar style: a cool, minimalist, effects-laden approach, owing more to post-punk notables like John McGeoch of Magazine and Siouxsie and the Banshees, or U2's The Edge, than the full-on rock 'n' roll of Captain Sensible or Brian James.

The lyrics describe the thrill and trepidation felt at the beginning of an affair, with a melodramatic flamboyance sure to satisfy the most ardent Anne Rice reader: 'I experience the most exquisite pain / A thousand whispers seem to say / I light a candle to you and I pray.'

Though it's an excellent pop song and a well-deserved hit, I prefer the single B-side 'Nightshift', which showed the band could still knock out raw tuneful punk without all the expensive-sounding bells and whistles. The 10' single also included the ludicrous novelty country song, 'Would You': featuring a guest vocal from Viv Mason (Rat's girlfriend and, later, wife), showing the band hadn't completely relinquished their absurd sense of humour.

'There'll Come a Day' (Roman Jugg / Bryn Merrick / Rat Scabies / Dave Vanian)

With its fuzzy signature guitar riff and minor-key organ accompaniment, this harks back to such Naz Nomad and the Nightmares influences as The Electric Prunes and Strawberry Alarm Clock – that strain of mid-1960s garage R&B, just edging into psychedelia, memorably anthologised on Lenny Kaye's seminal compilation, 'Nuggets' (1972).

On this largely Jugg-composed song (On *Phantasmagoria*, the principle songwriters are given first credit), the bluesy A minor verse (slightly reminiscent of The Monkees' '(I'm Not Your) Steppin' Stone' (1966)) gives way to the more harmonically adventurous chorus chords of B7/E/E minor, over a solid B bass pedal note. Vanian's lead vocal mirrors this, staying largely on a monotone B, while the backing vocals move in a soaring counterpoint. The lyrics are somewhat throwaway, more overwrought emoting for the Anne Rice crowd, where 'Fear grips your heart' and 'The torch of love is a burning flame' etc. It's all fine standard pop song nonsense, but we know The Damned can do better. Nevertheless, overall, the song is a decent pastiche of a style they clearly know and love. Unfortunately, once again, the production lets the track down, sapping out a lot of the life, rendering it somewhat flat and antiseptic. Everything's clean and precise, but there's little excitement, the track dragging its heels for an overlong 4:15, with Rat, in particular, sounding like he's playing in his sleep. I'd recommend hunting out the BBC session version from the same year, which shows how good the song could sound played with The Damned's customary verve and passion, unbound by major label commercial standards.

'Sanctum Sanctorum' (Dave Vanian / Roman Jugg / Bryn Merrick / Rat Scabies)

Almost all of *Phantasmagoria* is steeped in windswept, ghostly atmospherics, but it is on this ambitious Vanian-led multi-part ballad of love and loss that the album finally dives headlong into full-blown Gothic melodrama. A cathedral organ playing an introductory theme sets the scene, as ominous thunder sounds in the background. At around 90 seconds in, the grand, portentous organ chords succumb to a sorrowful piano in C minor, over which Vanian gently murmurs the opening verse – which finds our narrator unable to sleep, haunted by the past: 'I can't tear away from the night / It holds the seed of a memory.' The song gathers momentum, Merrick's bass making a tentative entrance, and Vanian's baritone becoming more resonant as he recalls his fledgling relationship's passion; regrettably throwing in more of the overwrought lyrical cliches that infest *Phantasmagoria*: 'The fire burned deep behind your eyes / I knew a kiss would paralyse.'

Nevertheless, as the lyric intensifies, the music builds, the drums moving from 4/4 time to a swinging 6/8, giving this section a feel akin to classic Tin Pan Alley torch songs such as Gene Pitney's 'A Town Without Pity' (1961). The music sweeps dramatically along on a tide of synth strings and Rat's cavernously-reverberating snare, the lyric recalling a 'love like a carnival's runaway ride', before the memory turns sour; and as the narrator muses 'Sometimes angels can be devils too /It's true of you', we return to the pensive C minor piano theme. It seems the object of his affections is gone, and there are dark hints that she may have also abandoned this mortal coil – 'The ghost of a call', 'The moments die', 'Drowned in your kiss' – and it's his destiny for her memory to haunt him forever, not unlike the narrator of Edgar Allen Poe's 'The Raven' (1845): surely the benchmark for all ballads of doomed Gothic romance. As a poet, Vanian isn't going to challenge Poe, but – some hackneyed lines aside – 'Sanctum Sanctorum' is an enjoyable piece of over-the-top drama and one of *Phantasmagoria*'s more successful ventures into Gothic excess.

'Is It a Dream' (Rat Scabies / Roman Jugg / Dave Vanian / Bryn Merrick / Captain Sensible)

Perhaps the most straight-ahead pop song on the album, 'Is It A Dream', is also the only one dating back to Captain Sensible's tenure, having been played live and recorded for a BBC radio session back in the first half of 1984. The Captain gets his only *Phantasmagoria* writing credit here, but we can assume from the name order that it's largely Rat's work. A fine piece it is, too: very much a 1960s throwback, lightweight but nicely constructed, packed with hooks and irresistibly melodic.

After a catchy opening piano riff, it settles into a solid mid-tempo groove, crunchy guitar chords supporting, with a keyboard melody doubled at octaves. The chord structure is simple, with both verse and chorus oscillating between

G and C, with a brief A minor bridge, focussing the listener's attention on Vanian's bold and strongly sung vocal melody.

The lyrics – very much from the Syd Barrett school – see our narrator speaking in surreal non-sequiturs: 'Standing in line like a parking meter', 'I know a man who's really awful nice – he isn't here' etc. Only in the middle eight does any unexpected harmonic development occur as a series of rising diminished chords reflect the lyric's mounting anxiety: 'Then, suddenly, like a fly in a cup of tea / I'm stirred and no longer free.' Over this same chord sequence, Roman unleashes some unquestionably 1980s-sounding lead guitar: all processed distortion, shredding runs and vibrato bar dive-bombs, showing the band weren't immune to Eddie Van Halen's all-pervasive influence on that decade's rock guitarists.

It's a pretty great pop record, although, again, I'd recommend looking up the BBC session version, which features much livelier work from Scabies and Merrick, a more traditionally heroic guitar solo from Sensible, and some heavy 'Itchycoo Park'-style phasing over the final chorus – rendering the album version slightly stodgy in comparison. Nevertheless, released as the third single, backed with fun – if inessential – live covers of The Trogg's 'Wild Thing' and (a rather garbled version of) Sex Pistols' 'Pretty Vacant', 'Is It A Dream' climbed to number 34 in the UK: a very decent showing.

'Grimly Fiendish' (Roman Jugg / Dave Vanian / Bryn Merrick / Rat Scabies / Doctor (Clive Thomas))

The Damned's first major-label single was recorded prior to the album sessions, with producer Bob Sargeant, at the helm, giving it a slightly different sound to the rest of *Phantasmagoria* – although it fits nicely into the running order. Written by Roman Jugg and named after Leo Baxendale's bungling cartoon villain, Grimly Feendish, the song is atypical for The Damned, tapping into the same peculiarly British blend of music hall jaunt and wistful, dark overtones heard on the likes of The Kinks' 'Sunny Afternoon' (1966) or Madness' 'Tomorrow's (Just Another Day)' (1983).

A piano motif doubled on synth harpsichord carries it along with some tastefully restrained guitar work. The melody is strong, weaving its way around an arresting E minor chord sequence. The lyrics appear to relate directly to the aforementioned would-be super-villain. However, rather than take an overtly humorous tone, they portray the character with sympathy and pathos; a soul to be pitied rather than laughed at: 'Simply fiendish, a child caught in a grown-up world / No lies convince the court.' After verse two, a veritable choir acting as a judgemental Greek chorus, supplant Vanian's vocal with their refrain of 'Bad lad, bad boy' over the chords of D and A: a section rather blatantly pinched from the 'Love love love long' middle eight of The Who's 'Our Love Was' (1967). Moving on, Vanian shifts to his higher register, as the narrative voice shifts to first-person, our protagonist answering his accusers: 'Let me get the story straight / You never gave me a break.' But his pleas are to no avail, as the third person voice returns, in a less sympathetic tone: 'Grimly Fiendish, we'll send you back where you belong'. After another choral refrain, a horn section plays the song out, bright marching band cornets giving way to sleazy muted wah-wah trumpet.

It's a fun, imaginative delve into baroque pop territory, which harks back to the 1960s while foreshadowing the mid-1990s Britpop movement. The single – backed with a pre-album recording of 'Edward The Bear' – reached number 21 in the UK, giving The Damned their biggest hit since 1979, re-establishing them as a serious commercial prospect.

'Edward the Bear' (Roman Jugg / Rat Scabies / Bryn Merrick / Dave Vanian)

Roman Jugg takes the lead vocal here, giving Syd Barrett's naïve psychedelic pop a 1980s makeover, ending up not a million miles from an indie-pop more often associated with someone like The Teardrop Explodes. The original version was recorded with Bob Sargeant as the B-side to 'Grimly Fiendish'. This new Jon Kelly production trims the running time to a compact 3:38 and also – inevitably – adds a slightly sterile 1980s sheen. The distinctive pulsing keyboard part (reminiscent of The Who's 'Won't Get Fooled Again' (1971)) underpinning the single version is still present, though a saxophone riff bearing a resemblance to Go West's 'We Close Our Eyes' (1985), all but drowns it out. This slight embarrassment aside, it's a pleasing listen, with Jugg's guitar jangling tastefully, adding some moderate rock muscle where required. His voice – though obviously lacking Vanian's iconic presence – has a pleasingly Barrett-like quality, which suits the song to a tee, backed up by some delightfully corny 'Ooh la la la' chorus harmonies.

The lyrics are by and large a cryptic rumination on a perplexing relationship, the chorus repeatedly asking, 'Who's the sucker now?'. Verse one, however, takes quite a different tone, echoing the works of A. A. Milne and Lewis Carroll, and tapping into the same vein of wistful nostalgia for a peculiarly British childhood, so often heard in UK pop of the mid-to-late 1960s: 'Shadows fall on the places we used to play / My toys have all been packed away / The rocking horse rocks in its box.' In keeping with the band's fascination for vintage UK comics, another reference to Corporal Clott (previously mentioned in 'The History Of The World') provides a nice piece of continuity.

Not the most essential *Phantasmagoria* track then, but a fine pop song and a nice break from the slightly over-egged atmospherics characterising much of the album.

'The Eighth Day' (Rat Scabies / Roman Jugg / Dave Vanian / Bryn Merrick)

An opening wash of sombre synths and eerie guitar harmonics suggests we're in for another exercise in brooding drama. Then suddenly, Rat's stomping rhythm kicks into an unexpectedly driving, excitable pop track, similar in feel to The Rolling Stones' classic, 'Let's Spend The Night Together' (1967). The solid, pounding drums and Merrick's lively melodic bass line do most of the heavy lifting. Aside from a fine, tuneful solo, Jugg's lead guitar mainly adds splashes of colour, with simple single notes or double stops that sustain and edge into harmonic feedback. A clean, muted rhythm guitar doubles the bass, and occasional synth-harpsichord flourishes retain a hint of gothic sensibility in what is otherwise a punchy, soulful pop record.

The lyrics are quite another matter, depicting the modern world in apocalyptic terms; the paradise built in creation's seven days, now a waking nightmare of man-made environmental crises, fear, war and rabid nationalism: 'Dancing dead are knocking at my door / In acid rain they came to mourn / To raise the flag, to raise the tune.' Music in the bright-sounding key of G major accompanies this bleak vision, but The Damned generate musical tension by hanging mainly on the chord of D (the dominant 5th of G) throughout the verse, which is only released when returning to the G tonic for the chorus. A brief post-chorus minor-key passage reflects the lyric's dark tone, but otherwise, the overall sound is determinedly upbeat: a really effective juxtaposition of moods, making 'The Eighth Day' a definite album highlight and showing that the band are more than capable of creating atmospheric pop without always resorting to the most obvious theatrics.

'Trojans' (Bryn Merrick / Roman Jugg / Rat Scabies / Dave Vanian)

The album concludes with only the second entirely instrumental track to feature on a Damned LP, after 'Smash It Up (Part 1)'. 'Trojans' represents an unusual direction: nearly five minutes of keyboard-laden meanderings in three movements, sounding more akin to a Jean-Michel Jarre synth-scape or the electronic film scores of Jan Hammer or Vangelis, than to anything normally associated with The Damned.

Opening with Rat's drum rhythm played at a glacial crawl, the first section is an ocean of synth shimmers, subtle guitar swells and tinkling high piano notes, all very atmospheric, never threatening anything like a melody. At around 2:20, a crashing gong (a common feature of the prog era, but rarely heard on anything punk-related) heralds a wistful solo piano theme, soon underscored by synth cello. The rhythm returns at double its previous pace, Gary Barnacle taking another soaring sax break. At 3:40, the pace doubles, Bryn's bass and Roman's tastefully restrained power chords holding down a solid G pedal note, as shifting piano chords ring out dramatically. As the key changes to B flat, synth arpeggios overlay the theme. This section was used for a time as the closing theme of Channel 4's weekly American football show. With another crash of the gong and with Scabies' drums getting ever more frantic, the track fades out, bringing to a conclusion an album packed with great ideas, but dominated by a production style proving to be commercially lucrative but somewhat artistically stifling.

Anything (1986)

Personnel:
Dave Vanian: Lead vocals
Roman Jugg: Guitars, keyboards and backing vocals
Bryn Merrick: Bass guitar and vocals
Rat Scabies: Drums
Additional personnel:
Blue Weaver: Keyboards
Paul 'Shirley' Shepley: Keyboards
Paul 'Wix' Wickens: Keyboards
Suzie O'List: Backing vocals
Kurt Holm: Trumpet
Recorded at Puk Recording Studios, Denmark
Produced and engineered by Jon Kelly
Additional engineering: Henrik Nilsson, Lance Phillips and Alan O'Duffy
Mixed by Nigel Walker and Ken Thomas
Record label: MCA
Released: December 1986
Highest chart position: UK: 40
Length: 41:00
Current edition: 2009 double CD expanded remastered reissue on Universal
Records.

The unprecedented success of *Phantasmagoria* and its singles, had made
The Damned household names, but also left MCA hungry for more product.
This demand was temporarily sated at the January 1986 release of the standalone single, 'Eloise'. Vanian had a long-standing desire to cover Barry Ryan's
1968 orchestral pop epic, and with a major label recording budget, the band
were finally able to do justice to the song in all its preposterous, bombastic
glory. Backed with the moody, Doors-ish 'Temptation', and a great cover of
the John Barry Seven's kitsch classic, 'Beat Girl' (the theme song to the 1959
teensploitation movie of the same name, starring Adam Faith), it was a huge
hit, reaching number 3 in the UK.

Since *Phantasmagoria*'s release, the band had had no break in their
promotional schedule, and now, with their popularity at an all-time high,
MCA decided it was time for another album. Unfortunately, as had happened
nine years earlier, the band had had no time to write material for the album
they were obliged to provide. Of the nine songs that make up *Anything*,
only 'In Dulce Decorum' had been demoed in advance. Everything else was
worked up from scratch in the studio: a time-honoured major label practice,
not only vastly wasteful but which also places unreasonable pressure on
the often fragile creative process. The Damned had a three-year run-up to
Phantasmagoria, with Roman emerging as a strong writer and the others all
having plenty of time and space to hone their ideas. Now, they were expected

77

to repeat or even top that success in a sterile studio environment, expenses mounting with every passing minute.

The label chose PUK: a 32-track all-digital residential studio in rural Denmark, partly for its then-cutting-edge sound but mainly as a way to keep Vanian present and engaged. His tendency to vanish at key moments as *Phantasmagoria* was recorded, had been noted. So the plan was to place the band where there was nowhere to wander off to; a plan Vanian promptly foiled for the first month by not turning up at all.

The fraught recording began with Roman Jugg alone working on backing tracks, Rat and Bryn eventually joining him. Dave finally showed up, completely unprepared, scrambling lyrics together. Producer Jon Kelly returned, padding out the rather thin material with even more bombast. Somehow they completed the record, and, preceded by the title track single, *Anything* came out in December 1986.

The sleeve – featuring a colourful woodcut design on the front and a photograph of the band decked out in a heck of a lot of black leather in front of a fairground ride's bright neon glow – suggested a move away from *Phantasmagoria*'s more explicitly gothic monochrome imagery, with MCA likely feeling that leather-clad rockers would appeal more to the American mainstream than that album's ashen-faced frock-coated dandy wastrels would. The fairground theme continued inside the lavish gatefold, with zany hall-of-mirrors band photos and a pop-up black and white band shot – an extravagant gimmick which either indicated MCA's confidence in the album or served as a distraction from a lacklustre record with fancy packaging, depending on your viewpoint.

Reaching number 40 in the UK and spawning three top 40 singles, *Anything* didn't do badly at all. But it had gone massively over budget, and after its predecessor's success, a palpable air of disappointment surrounded *Anything*, with MCA losing confidence in the band, who in turn became disillusioned with the major-label treadmill.

In November 1987, 'In Dulce Decorum' was the album's fourth released single, stalling at 72 in the UK, followed by the ominously-titled compilation album, *The Light at the End of the Tunnel*. Some effort was made to work on songs for another record, but in June 1988, MCA dropped The Damned. The impetus to continue was gone. Instead of promoting new music, the band began playing retrospective shows, with Brian James and Captain Sensible returning to perform classic material. Then, in May 1989, it was announced that The Damned would be splitting up.

'Anything' (Roman Jugg / Rat Scabies / Bryn Merrick / Dave Vanian)
As the album's opening song, title track and inaugural single, there's a lot riding on 'Anything', as the song to define our expectations of both the LP and this era of The Damned's career. Does the song live up to the weight of this responsibility? Er... sort of. The song has the clear outline of a classic two-and-a-half-minute Damned rock n' roller, and it's not a stretch to imagine it

played at *Machine Gun Etiquette* tempo with real fire and passion. However, this being a big-budget major label 1986 recording, the song is slowed down, padded out to a bloated 4:48, and bedecked with numerous extraneous production gimmicks.

The result sounds less like the Damned we know, and closer to Billy Idol's contemporary work: Idol, a fellow alumnus of London's class of '76, who by applying a slight edge of punk snottiness and danger to an otherwise slick, airbrushed stadium rock sound, became a US superstar. Jugg's guitar in particular, with its palm-muted chugging and chiming arpeggiated hook, is reminiscent of Steve Stevens' work on Idol's 'White Wedding' (1982). As on *Phantasmagoria*, a strict metronomic tempo robs Rat's playing of much of the spontaneity and elasticity, which made it so exciting. It's a solid, driving performance but lacks the nuance, flair and dynamics of his best playing, compounded by additional percussion, and smothered in gated reverb: that staple of 1980s drum recording, popularised by Phil Collins' 'In The Air Tonight' (1981). There are also the prominent backing vocals of Suzie O' List: an accomplished session singer who'd previously worked with such mainstream acts as Spandau Ballet and Eurythmics. Her voice is fine and soulful but out of place on a Damned record; and her inclusion smacks of Jon Kelly simply throwing every commercial element he could think of, into the mix, in the hope of a hit emerging.

The track's real saving grace is Dave Vanian's vocal: a truly commanding performance, with a hint of Elvis Presley's lip curl, a good dash of Jim Morrison's whiskey-soaked croon, and a large serving of Iggy Pop's mad-dog snarl. Vanian's enthusiasm really carries the song: impressive given the album sessions' unhappy circumstances. Indeed, the lyrics – with their refrain of 'Anything is better than this' – seem to be borne out of frustration with the band's situation: Vanian's goading 'I could never be what you need in me' seeming like a direct shot at the label executives trying to force-fit The Damned onto their cookie-cutter pop conveyor belt.

The single – backed with the atmospheric-but-directionless noodling of 'The Year of the Jackal' and aided by a somewhat puzzling video featuring Vanian singing in the shower while his bandmates eat a medieval banquet at a flying table – reached number 32. This would once have been notable, but compared to 'Eloise's spectacular performance, it must've seemed a flop and undoubtedly set off alarm bells at MCA. Still, as an album opener, it's pretty solid and stands up as one of the more completely realised songs on a, frankly, half-baked record.

'Alone Again Or' (Bryan Maclean)

The second song (but third single) was a cover of Love's woozy, flamenco-tinged orchestral pop masterpiece originally recorded in 1967 for the seminal *Forever Changes* LP; Love's single of it released in 1968.

Roman Jugg began the backing track while waiting for his unreliable bandmates; the verse one lyrics – 'I won't forget all the times I've waited patiently for you / And you'll do just what you choose to do' – perhaps ringing an ironic bell somewhere in his subconscious. Rat, arriving next, had apparently never heard the original and took it to be a Jugg original: wishful thinking during those inspiration-barren sessions.

This version recreates Love's arrangement almost note for note, although its subtleties are largely sacrificed at the altar of 1980s production. The distinctive Spanish guitar intro is present and correct, albeit played on an electric, swathed in glossy chorus, and the string arrangement is recreated on synthesizer, while Kurt Holm's Mariachi trumpet solo is authentic. A few minor lyric and vocal phrasing tweaks add nothing and are slightly jarring if you're familiar with Love's recording: one can't help wondering whether these were deliberate or merely misremembered, although that would seem strange considering everything else was reproduced so accurately.

In April 1987, the track was issued as a single, against the band's wishes. They felt that releasing another cover so soon after 'Eloise', was not a good move. Somewhat short-sightedly, it was backed with a live recording of 'In Dulce Decorum': the studio version of which would be the next single, and promoted with an expensive and utterly ridiculous video. Shot in the US, it featured the band in spaghetti western garb, Vanian sporting a silly moustache and dressed as a Mexican bandito, while a flamenco dancer twirls, and a big rig truck whips up a lot of dust. Clearly, director, Gerard De Thame, had taken all his cues from the music and none from the lyrics: an enigmatic portrait of a failing relationship. Nevertheless, the single climbed to 27 in the UK, becoming The Damned's last top forty single to date.

'The Portrait' (Roman Jugg, Rat Scabies, Bryn Merrick, Dave Vanian)

Less a song, more a piece of incidental mood music, 'The Portrait' would sound more at home underscoring a TV melodrama than it does in the middle of a Damned album. That said, it's quite an affecting ditty, scored for piano and synth strings, the sound of lapping waves overdubbed. The main theme utilises an unusual and evocative chord progression of Em/F/Dm/E, leaving the key uncertain until the next section lands firmly in A minor. If rendered as a brief interlude, it would be a nice palette cleanser, but for all its tinkling prettiness, it doesn't really go anywhere, and at 3:51 in length, feels like Roman (surely the only Damned member on it) padding out the album in the absence of his colleagues. At one time, the band would've fit two whole songs into the time given to this pleasant-but-pointless meander. Now, it seems that the goal was simply to fill up the album by any means necessary: a rather sad state of affairs.

'Restless' (Roman Jugg / Rat Scabies / Bryn Merrick / Dave Vanian)

Here we turn back towards the moodier, more gothic *Phantasmagoria* sound. However, while that album's atmospherics were consistently underpinned through solid pop songcraft and a carefully structured coherence, 'Restless' comes across as overlong, overproduced and under-composed.

The lyrics tell a story of sorts, the narrator relating his difficult upbringing and his troubled adulthood, which has seen him engage in unspecified nefarious activity – 'Walking in the footsteps of the beast' – all the time reminding us that he's still 'Too damned restless'. It's a rather vague and unsatisfying narrative, taking forever to tell us very little. Similarly, the music develops little over the track's five minutes. Rat's busy, tom-heavy drums churn away as Roman's heavily-chorused guitar clangs out the E minor and F chords upon which almost the whole song is based. At around 2:16, the drums cease briefly, Jugg playing an Am9 arpeggio which appears to herald a new section. But a few seconds later, we're back to the same old two-chord churn. Suzie O' List's backing vocals sound no less out of place than on the title track, and while Vanian does his best to inject drama and mystique, there's little discernible melody for him to work with.

A dud then, on which no amount of noisy, dated production can drown out the sound of the barrel bottom being scraped.

'In Dulce Decorum' (Roman Jugg / Rat Scabies / Bryn Merrick / Dave Vanian)
Side two of the original LP provides a little more substance, kicking off with this strident anti-war statement. Taking its title from Wilfred Owen's harrowing depiction of World War I trench warfare, *Dulce et Decorum Est* – which in turn takes its title from a longer quote by Roman poet, Horace, which translates as 'It is sweet and fitting to die for one's country' – the song takes the form of a soldier's letter home to his mother, powerfully conveying his sense of futility and naked fear.

The track opens with a patriotic Winston Churchill speech, contrasting starkly with the realities of war as described by the narrator: forced to kill unknown enemies who, seen up close, are just 'a man or boy who is just like me'; left so traumatised that 'If I could ever sleep again / I know until the end of time I'd hear their screams of pain'. It's hard-hitting and a welcome change from the prior album's relatively vacuous songwriting. Unfortunately, the instrumental accompaniment doesn't quite match the lyric's power. Instead of tapping into the rich, dark psychedelic garage punk vein that fuels The Damned's finest work, there's a distinct whiff of U2 in the air here, with Roman's heavily-treated guitar, chiming minimalistically over a slightly awkward funk shuffle, the chosen key forcing Vanian into his upper register, to strain uncomfortably in a way recalling Bono's histrionically overwrought style. U2 were very much in the ascendant at the time, so it's perhaps understandable that edging towards their sound would seem like an astute commercial move, but for the long-established and highly distinctive Damned, it seemed a bit obvious and unnecessary. The chorus refrain of 'To say in God we trust, not for this' reasserts the band's 1960s pop influences, with a strong melody and nifty, almost Beatlesque harmonies. But overall, the track is marred through the all-pervading influence of Ireland's premium purveyors of stadium angst: a shame really, as this is the album's strongest lyric, by some way.

Belatedly issued as a single – to accompany the *Light at the End of the Tunnel* compilation – 'In Dulce Decorum' limped to 72 in the UK. But that wasn't bad for the fourth single from a sub-par album, especially since the song's live version had already appeared, as the 'Alone Again Or' B-side, earlier in the year.

'Gigolo' (Roman Jugg / Rat Scabies / Bryn Merrick / Dave Vanian)

'Gigolo' takes its title, intro and chorus basis from Syd Barrett's 'Gigolo Aunt' (1970). In turning back to their trusty psychedelic-era influences, The Damned produced a power-pop gem, harking back to the catchiest moments of their *Strawberries* album. Granted, the lyrics appear to mean little beyond a vague condemnation of duplicity, but they are packed with interesting images and pop culture references, including Roger Moore (who had recently stepped down from the James Bond role, as acknowledged in Jugg's brief Bond theme guitar quote), and Vanian's inspiration: 'The prince of darkness from the horror flicks'. The chorus of 'You know what I ain't, I ain't no gigolo aunt' is a direct riposte to Barrett's 'I know what you are, you are a gigolo aunt', cheekily using the same melody and chord progression.

After the ponderous two-minute intro (sensibly excised from the single), the song is both livelier and more melodic than Barrett's hazy shuffle. Based on just three chords, the song-proper is simplicity itself, and even Jon Kelly's normally intrusive production doesn't spoil things, adding extraneous keyboards here and there, and quotes from Ennio Morricone's theme for *The Good, The Bad and the Ugly* (1966) and John Barry's *You Only Live Twice* (1967). Otherwise, it's pretty straightforward: ringing chords, simple verse drums, a great, almost McCartney-ish bridge melody, and rich, jangling chorus guitars with hints of The Byrds, or even Tom Petty and the Heartbreakers.

'Gigolo' was a number 26 UK hit, helped by a silly video featuring Vanian in schoolmaster's robe and mortarboard, singing with a rabbit on his head while the rest of the band – dressed for the Napoleonic wars – are pelted with stuffed toys. The track showed that even in difficult circumstances, The Damned could still turn out the occasional absolute corker.

'The Girl Goes Down' (Roman Jugg / Rat Scabies / Bryn Merrick / Dave Vanian)

A fun, if inessential and somewhat long venture into campy 1960s-tinged exotica, 'The Girl Goes Down' is built on a sultry, hypnotic groove, with Jugg's reverberating spy-theme/surf guitar and occasional Farfisa organ bursts doubled with female backing vocals, bringing to mind The B-52's' 'Rock Lobster' (1978). It prompts a fine Vanian performance: in full lounge-lizard mode, delivering corny lines like 'She stalks like pussycat stalks' with a lascivious zeal, almost making you forget how daft they are. Nevertheless, once the novelty wears off, there's not much of a song to latch onto.

Lyrically, the gist is there's a mysterious girl, and she goes ... somewhere. Where? Not sure, but she's got very penetrating eyes! As you can imagine, stretching this premise out to 4:46 is a tall order, and like most the album's songs, 'The Girl Goes Down' would benefit from being shorn by about two minutes. But compared to the slim pickings elsewhere here, it is entertaining, and something a little different, while still recognisable as the Damned.

'Tightrope Walk' (Roman Jugg / Rat Scabies / Bryn Merrick / Dave Vanian)

Like 'The Portrait', this is hardly a rock track, scored as it is entirely for synthesizer, except for each bar's solitary bass drum thud and some rumbling timpani to keep Rat vaguely involved, and of course, Vanian's vocal.

A virtual orchestra of synth cello and violas sawing away ominously at staccato root notes, forms the basis, beneath fleeting melodic violin phrases and hints of piano and harpsichord, with various sound effects chiming in occasionally. There's a sense of striving for the cinematic tension of Bernard Herrmann's superb *Psycho* (1960) score, yet here, the motifs quickly become familiar and repetitive with little dynamic variation to build suspense, and the song merely plods along. At 2:36, a brief instrumental section loses the insistent cello throb, introducing lusher orchestration. But we're quickly back to the same old theme. After a final verse with the aforementioned timpani adding excitement, the track ebbs away in a flurry of fairground organ, echoing the lyric's circus setting. These describe the titular circus act's performance in a (rather heavy-handed) metaphor for life's perilous journey: 'The dizzying heights, the sound of your heart's like thunder / Measure your step or all of your plans may fall asunder.' To make sure we've got the message, the final verse spells it out: 'The safety net is your psyche / The wire, though imaginary, yes, it's very real.' Vanian – ever the thespian – sells it like a champion, but unfortunately, 'Tightrope Walk' remains uninspired and uninspiring, serving little purpose except to fill another four and a half minutes.

'Psychomania' (Roman Jugg / Rat Scabies / Bryn Merrick / Dave Vanian)

Taking its title and some lyric inspiration from the cult British horror movie about a motorcycle gang called The Living Dead – who commit suicide and return from the grave through a black magic ritual – 'Psychomania' reaffirms The Damned's fondness for spooky kitsch, and at least attempts to round off the album with a burst of energy. The lyrics - mainly a somewhat over-egged romantic evocation of hitting the open road on two wheels - avoid directly addressing the film's outlandish plot, but there are hints of the supernatural in lines like 'The pleasure of the beast coursing through our veins' and 'Tales of love, tales of terror / Ghost riders go hell for leather'. It is the album's fastest song, but far from representing a return to punk roots, it dives into the bland waters of the strident-yet-inoffensive rock inhabiting both countless 'Driving Anthems' compilations and innumerable American mid-west AM radio station playlists.

Ringing guitar chords, a nice melodic riff from Merrick, and Vanian's cry of 'Let's go!' (Haven't heard one of those for a while!), ushers in the rhythm: not the unpredictable aggression of yore, but a solid, unchanging, metronomic chug. Over this, a horn section dominates, playing a line rather blatantly lifted from Otis Redding's classic, 'Hard To Handle' (1968). After a brief chorus with layered vocal harmonies, Vanian delivers a verse over sparse kick and snare, with stabbing brass punctuations. Given a looser production – allowing the band's personality to assert itself more fully – this could've sounded akin to The Who's punchy, brass-laden rocker, 'The Real Me' (1973). Sadly, the rigid layers of 1980s pop polish prevented that from happening – keeping everything very clean. Roman lets loose with a ludicrous dive-bombing guitar solo: an opportunity to do the old guitar-impersonating-revving-motorbike trick, as performed by Todd Rundgren on Meat Loaf's 'Bat Out Of Hell' (1977) and Mick Mars on Motley Crue's 'Too Fast for Love' (1981). A middle eight with Hammond organ twiddles and angelic choral vocals, only strengthens the Meat Loaf/Jim Steinman comparison – the whole thing feeling cynically engineered by MCA to make the band more marketable in the US. But sadly, no amount of production airbrushing or fancy leather outfits would make The Damned appeal to the American heartland, and the hoped-for US breakthrough never came.

Not of This Earth/I'm Alright Jack & the Bean Stalk (1995)

Personnel:
Dave Vanian: Vocals
Rat Scabies: Drums, piano
Kris Dollimore: Guitar
Moose: Bass, backing vocals
Additional personnel:
James Taylor: Hammond organ
Alan Lee Shaw: Theme guitar, backing vocals
Glen Matlock: Bass on 'Tailspin' and 'Never Could Believe'
Recorded at Connie's Studio, Cologne. 'Tailspin' recorded at Jacob's Studio, Farnham; and Ratty's attic.
Produced by David M. Allen
Record label: Toshiba (Japan), Marble Orchard (UK), Cleopatra (US)
Released: November 1995 (Japan), April 1996 (UK), 1996 (US)
Highest chart position: uncharted
Running time: 42:34
Current edition: 2015 LP reissue on Trust No One Records.

Although The Damned had officially announced their break-up in 1989, there was still a remarkable amount of band activity into the early 1990s, with long and lucrative 'farewell' tours featuring Brain James, Captain Sensible and Paul Gray, performing back-catalogue material. Meanwhile, Roman Jugg and Bryn Merrick still participated in occasional Naz Nomad and the Nightmares shows, and also joined Dave Vanian in his new 1950s-inspired project: The Phantom Chords – within which Donagh O' Leary replaced Merrick after his drinking became problematic (Merrick sadly passed away in 2015, aged 56).

At the start of the US leg of the 1991 tour, Norfolk, Virginia's Skinnies Records released a new single, 'Prokofiev', under the Damned name; though in truth, the recording consisted of a loop from Iggy & The Stooges' 'Gimme Danger' (1973) with Brian James playing guitar over the top, and Rat adding tapes and sound effects: not exactly a 'proper' Damned record, then. James' participation in the reunion/farewell shows came to an abrupt halt when Sensible's onstage quip regarding Guns N' Roses mooted – and at the time hush-hush – cover of 'New Rose', caused offence. James threw down his guitar, stormed offstage, and left the band, apparently never to return, leaving the remaining members to conclude the tour without him.

As the tour wound to a close in 1992, it looked like the band was finally finished. But there was still Damned-related activity, like Guns n' Roses' 'New Rose' cover surfacing on 1993's *The Spaghetti Incident?* (Introducing The Damned to a whole new audience), and a steady stream of archive releases throughout the decade: the best of which was probably the 'Fun Factory' single – released on Sensible's Deltic label in 1990 – a superb psychedelic pop blast from the *Strawberries* sessions, featuring King Crimson's, Robert Fripp. However, with James having severed all ties with The Damned and Vanian and Sensible busy with their own ventures, it looked as if Rat would have to start again from scratch.

After some casting around, Rat settled into a trio with Jason 'Moose' Harris – formerly of Bradford folk-punk mavericks, New Model Army – and Alan Lee Shaw: a long-time Damned associate and occasional member of various Brian James bands. Scabies and Shaw started writing together, concocting a demo with which Scabies unsuccessfully attempted to woo Dave Vanian back into the fold. Undeterred, Scabies recruited lead guitarist Kris Dollimore: formerly of slightly punkish R&B rockers, The Godfathers. After working more on the songs, Scabies appealed again to Vanian. With The Phantom Chords failing to make much impact and a costly divorce looming, the singer agreed to come aboard. Although initially billed as The Damagement, with two original members present it was only a matter of time before they officially became the new Damned line-up.

This brand new Damned gigged from late 1993 to early 1995, playing old material and new songs written by Scabies and Shaw (the latter who left the band in 1994); they even recorded a Radio 1 session. Somewhere in this time frame, they ventured into the studio to record the new material with long-time Cure producer, David M. Allen – and it is at this point that the participants' stories diverge. Vanian maintains he was under the impression that the recordings were to be viewed as glorified demos, and only for Japanese release: a means of raising funds to record a 'proper' Damned album, with new songs and the possible return of Sensible. Scabies on the other hand, insists the tracks were always intended for the new Damned album, but that Vanian became disgruntled when Rat refused to give him credit on songs already written before Vanian joined the new line-up. We may never know the truth, but in any case, the dispute tore the band apart, creating bad blood that for a long time seemed to have permanently ended Scabies and Vanian's musical partnership.

Irrespective of Vanian's wishes, the recordings were released as a new Damned album, albeit in a confusing and haphazard fashion. It was initially issued in Japan (as planned) on the Toshiba label as *Not of This Earth*, with an elaborate lenticular CD cover depicting a verdant fantasy landscape, which created a cheeky animation when moved. It was then issued in the UK with the same cover art, but titled *I'm Alright Jack & the Bean Stalk*; and in the US as *Not of This Earth*, but with a different cover.

If the release strategy was confusing, the music within was no less baffling to anyone already familiar with the band's work. Granted, different Damned line-ups had produced a wide range of sounds, but there had always been a thread of continuity from album to album, even when circumstances and personnel had changed considerably in the intervening period. In contrast, *Not of This*

Earth sounds absolutely nothing like *Anything* and also bears little relation to the band's earlier eras, despite the familiar presence of Vanian's warm baritone and Scabies' frenetic drums.

With no Vanian writing input, the songs lack his trademark mystique and drama, and despite theoretically being co-written with Scabies, they also uniformly lack the pop sensibility Rat brought to earlier tracks like 'Wait for the Blackout' and 'The Eighth Day'. Instead, we have a set of fairly straight-ahead blues-based songs, which may aspire to mimic the raw directness of the Brian James era, but oddly end up more akin to Dollimore's former band, The Godfathers, even though they were written before he joined The Damned. Listening back, it's easy to understand Vanian's assertion – quoted in Kieron Tyler's book – that *Not of This Earth* 'wasn't a Damned album', as it really doesn't resemble the band. On the other hand, Dave was quite happy to sing these songs live with a band billed as The Damned for a couple of years, so whether he likes the album or not now, it deserves to be considered part of their catalogue. Nevertheless, with the band irrevocably splitting before the album was released, there was no hope of promoting it, and it sank without a trace: their first studio album to fail to chart since *Music for Pleasure*. This time, it seemed The Damned really were finished. However, it was only a year later that another very different version of the band emerged, as The Damned continued to refuse to die.

'I Need a Life' (Rat Scabies / Alan Lee Shaw)

The first new Damned album in nine years begins with a slow blues in 6/8, with Rat keeping time with snare rimshots and Dollimore indulging in lazy wah-wah noodling. Frankly, it's not the most promising start, but after one cycle through the chord sequence, a drum fill kicks things up several notches, and the band launches into some driving uptempo blues-rock. The immediate positive factor worth noting, is that both original members sound fantastic here and indeed throughout the album. Rat, in particular, is back to his nimble, inventive best, finally free from the strictures of 1980s over-production. Dollimore and Moose turn in perfectly adequate performances, and the energy level is good. Even British jazz-funk revivalist James Taylor – surprisingly – supplies some nice Hammond organ. The only problem is – and this will become the album's running theme – the song just doesn't cut it: an idiotically basic A blues riff is latched to a 12-bar structure that only slightly varies from convention, with not a hint of melody in sight. 'I Need A Life' is essentially generic, hard pub rock that would sound right at home as a Dr Feelgood B-side or buried on a late-1970s Pirates' reunion LP, but as the opening song of a Damned album, it is distinctly sub-par. The lyrics, too are paper-thin: a verse and a half of vague relationship angst and a chorus built on the old 'alone/phone' rhyme cliché – all serving more as filler than conveying any kind of meaning. Obviously, there's no rule saying rock 'n' roll has to mean anything: some of the greatest rock records ever made are practically gibberish. However, that gibberish tends to generate excitement, create mystique, or at least sound cool. But for all the accomplished punch of the performance here, 'I Need a Life' is ultimately rather empty.

'Testify' (Rat Scabies / Alan Lee Shaw)

'Testify' begins unpromisingly with muted blues picking, but once the 12-bar cycle is complete and the guitars hit a big G power chord, Rat's drums take the track in an unexpected direction. Rather than the usual hard-driving forward momentum, 'Testify' uses the old Stooges trick of basing the song on a circular drum pattern, something The Damned hadn't attempted since resurrecting 'Alone' for *Music for Pleasure*. The pattern Rat plays here is considerably more complex than anything Scott Asheton ever played on a Stooges record: a flailing, lurching spasm of crashes and syncopated snare hits, a flurry of toms punctuating every fourth bar – it sounds ready to collapse at any second, and really shouldn't work. But Scabies somehow pulls it off, providing a writhing restless backdrop for Dollimore's wall of power chords, and a full-voiced Vanian in booming southern preacher mode, recounting a life lived in sin, and urging his congregation to 'Fall to the ground upon your knees – testify!'. Vanian had subversively played the clergyman before, when the 1982 *Strawberries* stage show presented the set as a religious service, with vampiric Vanian clad in vicar's dog collar, accompanied by Goth nuns. It's a role he can still adopt to great effect even now: witness the mock-gospel call-and-response section of 2017's 'Daily Liar'. But here, he plays the part beautifully, bringing a sense of drama and gravitas to what is, essentially, just another twelve-bar blues.

Dollimore takes up the challenge, giving as wild a performance as he can muster, laced with feedback howls and pick-slides, and featuring a fierce wah-wah solo. His playing may lack the range and invention of Captain Sensible's or the inspired abandon of Brian James', but Dollimore has a good stab at causing a little Ron Asheton-style mayhem.

A decent track then, though certainly not strong enough to justify the 1997 *Testify* EP on Cleopatra: a seven-song CD including two pointless title track remixes, similar reworkings of other *Not of This Earth* songs, and a live recording of 'Looking At You' by the completely different 1985 Damned line-up – an unasked-for and unnecessary release, to be filed under 'For completists only'.

'Shut It' (Rat Scabies / Alan Lee Shaw)

More basic phoned-in twelve-bar blues, somewhat elevated by a powerful performance. In this case, it isn't quite a twelve-bar structure, a couple of the phrases drawn out a little longer, but we're still essentially listening to amped-up pub R&B trying to sound like the Stooges. In fact, the riff here sounds like a poor attempt at Ron Asheton's 'TV Eye' motif (*Funhouse* album (1970)), chopped in half and reduced to a simple blues-rock cliché, repeated ad nauseum. Dollimore does his best to enliven it, interspersing little fills and zipping up the octave occasionally. The rhythm section pushes the track forward, Rat's aggressive fills right on top of the beat, Moose's nifty walking bass lines adding much-needed harmonic interest, but the resulting track is still distinctly uninspiring. Once again, there's no discernible melody, and the lyrics are more of the same vague relationship anguish.

I'm inclined to place the blame for this sharp change in musical direction, largely on Alan Lee Shaw, simply because his presence in all but one of the songwriting credits coincides with it, but we'll never know for certain to what extent he masterminded this era of the band. Likewise, I should note I'm not at all sure what his performance contribution to this album was. He had officially left the band by the time it was recorded but is still credited with 'theme guitar', whatever that means. Anyway, whoever is responsible, 'Shut It' is thoroughly unremarkable. Cleopatra Inexplicably released it as a single in September 1996 – backed with a remix by German industrial pioneers, Die Krupps – and, unsurprisingly, it failed to ignite interest. Like the rest of the album's material, 'Shut It' has not been played live since 1995.

'Tailspin' (Rat Scabies / Alan Lee Shaw)
The bluesy feel continues on this intro, with Dollimore's shimmering tremolo guitar playing a smoky, jazz-like sequence of Am9/F7/B7aug9. Vanian's low, close-mic'ed intimate croon, adds to the verse's sultry after-hours feel; and for a moment, it feels as if the track may edge towards the darkly-atmospheric realms first explored in *The Black Album*'s more subdued moments. Then the chorus kicks in, transforming the song into a subtlety-free hard rock ballad ala late-1980s or early-1990s Alice Cooper (think 1989's 'Poison'), though less glossy and considerably less melodic.

The lyrics are more relationship angst (which seems to be the album's overriding theme) here with extra sexual tension, expressed through a series of rather excruciating cliches: 'My mind leaves my body when you brush against my skin / I shake and shiver, there's a fever all the time.' The chorus repeats the phrase 'I'm in a tailspin, and my head keeps burning', a chromatic descending riff representing this loss of control, which is a nice touch.

It's okay – faultlessly played and with a great Vanian lead vocal, but do we really listen to The Damned for adequate hard-rock balladry? Worthy of note is this track's bass, played by original Sex Pistols member Glen Matlock. It's a perfectly fine, though completely unremarkable, performance, showing no obvious reason why Matlock – rather than Moose – played the part. It's ironic that a collaboration between UK punk originators should produce a track that owes more to US radio rock than anything remotely punky.

'Not of this Earth' (Rat Scabies / Alan Lee Shaw)
Here the band dabble in another atypical sound: a kind of 1970s boogie-rock evoking a distinctly pre-punk, flared-trousered and long-haired sound.

Admittedly, The Damned often gave nods to classic pop, garage, psychedelia and even rockabilly, but this lurch into grubby biker boogie was a new, and not entirely welcome, turn. For a band that has drawn from pop's past with wide-ranging and impeccable taste, to make a record this similar to Dutch heavy rockers Golden Earring's 1973 hit, 'Radar Love', is a bit of an embarrassment. 'Not of This Earth' casts an unspecified person, who we are told is 'A liar ... a cheat ... a snake in the grass' and 'An evil heart'. It's an outpouring of accusations that don't really develop, getting tangled in confused images along the way: 'You wear the truth like a disease / There's no hole deep enough for you to please.' Well, it rhymes, but it doesn't really mean anything, does it? As with 'Tailspin', 'Not of This Earth' is capably performed, but the song is weak, and its style uncomfortably close to the turgid dinosaur rock that punk was designed to wipe out.

'Running Man' (Rat Scabies / Alan Lee Shaw)

More wah-wah blues noodling ushers in this utterly dull plod, which sounds not unlike a pub cover band misremembering an old ZZ Top song. There's really nothing positive I can say. Based on a churning C and F chord repetition, it's a tuneless wonder with idiotically banal lyrics, and with drearily indulgent guitar-twiddling dragging it out to nearly five minutes. Vanian tries and fails to sound enthusiastic – and with lyrics like 'Running man, you just can't stand / Running man, you just can't plan', who can blame him? Scabies, to his credit, plays some impressive fills, but the overall feel is so sluggish that even doubling the time for the final minute injects no life. In the context of even a sub-standard Damned record, this really is very poor.

'My Desire' (Rat Scabies / Alan Lee Shaw)

Thankfully, 'My Desire' picks up the pace, flying from the starting blocks with Scabies' absolutely explosive playing. Granted, the riff is yet more blues/rock for beginners; there's little by way of a melody; and the bridge is more-or-less lifted from Dead Or Alive's 1984 hit, 'You Spin Me Round (Like A Record)'. Nevertheless, it's a sprightly, enthusiastic performance which – at 2:45 in length – doesn't outstay its welcome. Given the speed, one might expect a hint of *Machine Gun Etiquette*, if not in quality, then at least in feel. However, fast and furious though 'My Desire' is, it's not in the least bit 'punk'; instead, leaning, once again, towards hard rock. In fact, between Dollimore's tight riffing and shrill lead squeals, and James Taylor's bluesy organ wig-out, the track seems more closely related to uptempo early-1970s Deep Purple – like 'Fireball' (1971) or 'Speed King' (1970) – than to the proto-hardcore punk and pop blend The Damned pioneered back in 1979.

The lyrics are more of the space-filling doggerel we've come to expect from Shaw (I can't quite bring myself to blame Scabies, however culpable he may actually be): our narrator is disillusioned with his relationship (verse one) and his town (verse two), causing him enough consternation to rhyme the word 'mind' with itself in the chorus. Still, for all its lazy lyrics and dinosaur rock tendencies, 'My Desire' is a lively and entertaining listen – which in the context of this record, is a real blessing.

'Never Could Believe' (Rat Scabies / Alan Lee Shaw)

If punchy brevity improved 'My Desire', 'Never Could Believe' is absolutely sunk by its drawn-out running time. Essentially it's just one not-very-interesting idea: an edited version of The Beatles' 'Dear Prudence' riff, repeated with varying dynamics and overlaid with indulgent solos, for nearly five minutes. The vocal meanders, never cohering into anything recognisable as a tune; and the lyrics are hippie drivel, aiming for profundity but missing by a country mile: 'You will find that this time around it's just another dream / Search your mind and you might find its way out of reach.' Even the usually exemplary Dave Vanian strains awkwardly in his upper register, not sounding great; and even though Glen Matlock (in his second appearance here) tries heroically to inject musical interest via some McCartney-esque melodic bass touches, the whole thing is an ill-conceived shambles unworthy of the Damned name.

'Heaven ... Can Take Your Lies' (Rat Scabies / Alan Lee Shaw)

We're back in blues-based hard rock mode here, with some stodgy mid-tempo early-1970s-style riffing, slightly enlivened by Scabies' driving performance, which noticeably accelerates in tempo but does include some unexpectedly funky snare work. Vanian sounds strong here, moving from a low, menacing snarl to a higher register sounding more powerful and controlled than it did on the previous track; and his delivery almost masks the clunky lyrics, which attempt to paint a portrait of a life unravelling, but get tangled up in their own nonsensical imagery: 'You light a blue paper from the power of one ... the cards in your pack all wild with contempt,' and so forth. It's pretty half-baked, and by about 90 seconds in, it's used up its meagre supply of ideas, leaving us to sit through another two minutes of Dollimore's repetitive blues noodling. There's also a tinny-sounding and rather sloppy rhythm guitar track, distractingly rattling away on the right side. Could this be Shaw's elusive 'theme guitar'? If so, I'm about as impressed with his guitar stylings as his songwriting.

'Shadow To Fall' (Rat Scabies / Alan Lee Shaw)

And we're back to the 'Radar Love' boogie-rock shuffle and a blues riff in A made up of the same three notes that formed the main 'Heaven ... Can Take Your Lies' motif – just played in a different order. But it is hammered out with vigour, and the intro shout of 'Oi! Cloth-ears!' shows the irreverent sense of humour so far conspicuous in its absence from this album. In a now-familiar pattern, the performances themselves – especially from Vanian and Scabies – are strong, but the song is weak, tuneless, and has lyrics that defy any semblance of meaning: 'Shadowed by life, well you never can tell / Fall down a hole and you burn in hell / Striptease yourself against a wall / And watch those shadows begin to fall.' A breakdown section at least brings a little difference, Taylor chimes in with some organ, and everyone works themselves into a frenzied crescendo. But it can't hide the fact that the song is basically interchangeable with several others here.

'No More Tears' (Rat Scabies / Alan Lee Shaw)

We might expect the reverb-and-tremolo-laden guitar intro that ushers in this subdued A minor blues to merely be a quiet prelude to another crunching hard-rock track: a move made a couple of times on this record. But here, the band commit to the mood, in the process creating something more interesting. A downbeat, soul-searching ballad with definite 1950s leanings, 'No More Tears' lives somewhere between *Phantasmagoria*'s darker moody atmosphericism and Chris Isaak's 1989 retro smash, 'Wicked Game', which works surprisingly well. The lyrics may not be profound or original, but at least they actually mean something, and Vanian sells them well in a heartfelt, nuanced performance. The arrangement is tasteful, the playing spare and subtle; and coming after so much boring, repetitive bluster, it's an unexpected and very welcome pleasure.

'Prokofiev' (Rat Scabies / Brian James)

'No More Tears' was the perfect opportunity to end the album on a high point: a possible reflective and thoughtful conclusion to an otherwise brash and one-dimensional record. Instead – for no reason I can fathom – we get a rehash of this aimless jam/experiment that barely justified its limited single release back in 1991. Brian James is credited as a writer but not performer, so we must presume his contributions have been overdubbed, although some of the noodling sounds eerily familiar. Though a sped-up loop from The Stooges' 'Gimme Danger' (1973) forms the basis of the entire track, they are still uncredited, and this version omits the apparently random Vanian vocal snatches on the original single A-side, and uses the even less interesting B-side instrumental version as its starting point. Listeners would be best to turn the album off after 'No More Tears', which would save them three and a half minutes of tedium. 'Prokofiev' is a frustratingly dull and unnecessary conclusion to this darkest of Damned chapters. Thankfully, there were better times ahead.

Grave Disorder (2001)

Personnel:
David Vanian: Vocals, theremin
Captain Sensible: Guitar, backing vocals
Patricia Morrison: Bass, backing vocals
Monty Oxy Moron: Keyboards, backing vocals
Pinch: Drums, backing vocals
Recorded at Mad Dog Studios, Burbank, California
Produced by David Bianco
Record label: Nitro
Released: August 2001
Highest chart position: uncharted
Running time: 57:35
Current edition: Nitro Records original CD release/2017 LP repress.

The *Not of this Earth/I'm Alright Jack* ... debacle would've been a sour note
to end the Damned saga on. But by December 1995 – even before its UK
release, and only a few months after the Dollimore/Moose line-up ground to
a halt – the seeds of a new Damned line-up were already being sown. Fate
(or a canny promoter) conspired to bill both Vanian's Phantom Chords and
Captain Sensible on the same London show. Though consistently excellent,
the 1950s-flavoured Phantom Chords had never really caught on commercially:
likewise Sensible; though his solo output remained wildly inventive and
entertaining, his time as a mainstream pop artist was well behind him. A
backstage chat turned into a tentative plan, and soon, gigs were being booked
for a new Damned-type band.

Initially billed as 'Dave Vanian & Captain Sensible ex-THE DAMNED' – before
finally assuming the official moniker when any litigation from Scabies failed to
appear – a few members came and went, including Paul Gray, briefly, before
a settled line-up finally emerged. Bassist, Patricia Morrison (Vanian's future
wife) – formerly of legendary Los Angeles punk combos, The Bags and The
Gun Club, and also UK Goth legends, The Sisters of Mercy – joined Vanian and
Sensible alongside drummer Andrew 'Pinch' Pinching of English Dogs: the
UK82 thrashers-turned-prog-metal headbangers. On keyboards came Laurence
Burrow, aka Monty Oxy Moron (later amended to Oxymoron), whose flair for
the whimsical, surreal and psychedelic, made him a natural Sensible ally.

1996 was a good year for a Damned comeback. Contrary to widespread
critical opinion, punk never died, but it did go off the radar in the late 1980s
– extreme hardcore and crossover thrash becoming the era's dominant punk
styles. However, in the US, the pioneering efforts of popular underground
acts like Husker Du, Fugazi and Bad Religion led to a mainstream punk
rediscovery (or rebirth, to many), starting with Nirvana's 1991 breakthrough,
which paved the way for Green Day, The Offspring, Rancid and many more. In
the UK, the likes of the powerful but melodic Snuff and Leatherface, usurped

extreme thrash's punk-scene dominance at the turn of the decade, and by the mid-1990s, a thriving young punk scene existed alongside the wildly-popular Britpop movement: itself partially drawing on classic UK punk and new wave. In the midst of this, 1996 marked the 20th anniversary of punk as we know it, and interest in the genre's originators was at an all-time high. The Sex Pistols overcame long-standing acrimony with the aptly named 'Filthy Lucre' tour, and countless lesser bands followed suit, reforming and making the most of the nostalgia. Acknowledging the trend, the Holidays In The Sun festival began in Blackpool, providing a huge platform for these classic (and not-so-classic) punk bands. Renamed Rebellion in 2007, the festival continues to this day, with bands new and old playing to a pan-generational audience. The Damned have headlined on numerous occasions.

The rejuvenated Damned soon established themselves as a formidable live presence: Vanian prowled the stage as menacingly as ever, and Sensible resumed his role of manic comic foil as if he'd never been away. Pinch might've lacked Rat's jazzy spontaneity but played with a power, precision and technical skill that ensured shows were fast and hard but stayed on the rails. On stage, Monty brought the band's psychedelic side to life, without ever diluting their punk intensity; and Patricia played the Gothic ice queen, counterbalancing Sensible's crazed antics, and perfectly complimenting Vanian's vampiric persona.

Initially, sets consisted of the hits and favourite album tracks, leaning heavily on the 1979-1982 era, with a healthy dash of Brian James songs, but nothing from the post-Captain era, except for 'Eloise'. The new-look Damned catered for the punk nostalgia appetite very successfully. But over time, the occasional new song sneaked into the setlist, suggesting there was more to this Damned incarnation than simply celebrating their legacy. Eventually, the band signed with US label, Nitro Records (owned by Dexter Holland, leader of perennially-mediocre-but-vastly-successful Orange County punks, The Offspring). The label's roster included a number of classic punk bands – like The Vandals, and noted Damned acolytes, TSOL; and newer bands such as AFI, who found a huge audience with their modern slant on The Damned's punk/goth blend – so the partnership made sense in terms of helping The Damned reach a broader, younger listenership.

The first new recording was for the compilation, *Short Music for Short People* (1999): a novel collection put together by 'Fat' Mike Burkett of L.A. punk band, NOFX, with 101 punk bands each contributing a sub-40-second song. While most opted for speedy three-chord rock, The Damned's 'It's a Real Time Thing' subverted expectations, being a 31-second burst of macabre horror ambience: a clear standout amidst some exalted company (Bad Religion, Green Day, The Misfits, Black Flag etc.)

In 2000, recording in the US for the first time, the band began work on a new album, with producer, David Bianco: at the time best-known for producing bands from the more polite end of the 'alternative rock' spectrum (Teenage

Fanclub, Primal Scream, Buffalo Tom etc.). The following year, they delivered *Grave Disorder*: a 13-song album, packaged in Vince Ray's retro horror comic art, with music combining elements of *Machine Gun Etiquette* punk, *Black Album* gothic rock and *Strawberries* power pop, while incorporating more contemporary sounds with varying degrees of success. Bianco's glossy, modern production was slightly at odds with the more 'classic' material, and the songwriting was perhaps not as consistently great as during the band's early-1980s peak, but overall, it was a far stronger effort than you could reasonably expect from a band in their 25th year. Easily the best product to bear the Damned name since *Phantasmagoria*, *Grave Disorder* swept memories of the terribly-lacklustre *Not of This Earth* aside; and though *Grave Disorder* didn't chart, it certainly took the band to new places, including a stint on The Vans Warped Tour: the hugely-popular punk and skateboarding package tour. Having already established themselves as a formidable live band, the new-look Damned now had a record that proved they were still a powerful creative force.

'Democracy?' (Captain Sensible)

A returning Captain Sensible wastes no time in making his presence felt with this barnstorming opener. Rattling along at 'Love Song'-like pace, with an almost metallic chugging precision, thanks in no small part to Pinch's powerhouse drums, 'Democracy?' gives a nod to the band's past, while showing they were more than capable of crossing swords with the younger melodic hardcore bands. It rides on a classic Sensible riff, combining crunching power chords with ringing open strings. The verse's rein in for the dynamics – Pinch's drums reduced to an impatient tom-tom bubbling, while Monty's unobtrusive organ chords back up Vanian's vocal. The term 'unobtrusive' also fits Morrison's bass style. Not given to Paul Gray-style flights of fancy – and with a much less trebly/aggressive tone than the band's previous bassists – her playing locks tight with the drums, filling out the sound without seeking to be the centre of attention.

For a band who once proclaimed their lack of interest in politics, the bold 'Democracy?' is a bitterly cynical rejection of the democratic process as an agent for positive change, written at a time when the wave of optimism that swept much of the UK as Tony Blair's Labour government finally ended seventeen years of Tory rule, had begun to subside. Watching Blair and company reveal themselves to be little more than Tories in different coloured ties, Sensible writes: 'Did you notice that just recently in London town, the flags all waved? / The people smiled a lot, the world was right / But now it seems that nothing's changed'; eventually concluding: 'Revolution changes nothing and voting changes even less / 'Cos it's only time you're wasting on democracy.' It's a pretty bleak outlook, but one that reflects the feeling of many who hoped for real change after the Thatcher years; and one that would soon seem especially prescient when, despite massive public outcry, Blair persisted in taking the UK to war against Iraq in the wake of 9/11.

The chorus moves to the key of A, with a big, poppy lead vocal and great wordless vocal harmonies. (Backing vocals are a particular strength of this line-up, with all members contributing, allowing for more ambitious vocal arrangements). Having established these elements, the structure is simple: alternating verse and chorus, with Sensible inserting a blistering wah-wah solo after chorus two, some fierce fills interspersed in the final verse. The whole performance zips by with unflagging, explosive energy before slowing to a crashing rock 'n' roll ending. It's a fantastic, fearsome recording of a great song, which soon found itself as a regular setlist fixture alongside the old favourites.

'Song.com' (Captain Sensible / David Vanian)
If 'Democracy?' had made any listeners worry that The Damned had become po-faced, then their fear would surely have been dispelled by 'Song.com'. Opening with Morrison's rumbling bass riff and Pinch's archetypal surf rhythm, the tone is deceptively menacing at first, similar to the dark surf-punk of Orange County's Agent Orange, especially with Sensible's power chords and Vanian's cry of 'Surf's up!'. But as soon as we hit the verse, any air of danger vanishes, and we're in bubblegum territory with a big goofy pop melody. The song's premise – lyrics crammed with daft (and now very dated) internet-surfing references set to music crammed with surf signifiers – is as simple as it is silly, and was often singled out for derision among reviewers, even as they praised the album overall. I do understand the derision: there's an air of 'old punks writing about a current phenomenon in order to sound relevant' about it; and lyrics like 'Chatting with a new-made chum, doesn't know I look a bum / She thinks that I'm six foot three, look like Jason Priestley' aren't going to be to everyone's taste. But to these ears at least, it's so ridiculous that it somehow works. Vanian sings with a deadpan suaveness, and the surf music cliches are layered on with infectious glee. Sensible accompanies the verses with clean, vibrola-laden chords, sneaking in some Dick Dale-style reverb-drenched tremolo picking. Monty takes a wild Hammond organ solo, Pinch inserts rattling tom rolls straight out of The Surfaris' 'Wipe Out' (1963), and the elaborate vocal arrangement pastiches The Beach Boys and Jan and Dean. For all the corny 1960s references at its core, the track is still hard-driving melodic punk. Is it meaningful? Ground-breaking? Life-changing? No. Is it fun? Yes indeed.

'Thrill Kill' (Captain Sensible / Pinch)
Fun isn't really on the agenda for 'Thrill Kill', sadly. It's dark and brooding, as we've come to expect, but instead of drawing on vintage horror and gothic melodrama, the song aims for something grittier and more urban. Certainly there are elements echoing *The Black Album*'s spookier moments: such as a tense bass line and spy movie chords recalling 'Twisted Nerve', and Monty's eerie discordant piano and synth harking back to '13th Floor Vendetta'. But

a few heavy-handed touches – presumably added to give the track a more contemporary feel – compromise the chilling atmosphere: including intrusive violent-sounding movie dialogue samples, and a weirdly-processed guitar dominating the main hook. Most unforgivable though, is the snare drum sound, which on this track alone (thankfully) has a high, resonant tone then hugely popular among nu-metal acts like Linkin Park and Papa Roach. In fact, Pinch's drums are a poor fit throughout: an overly-busy funk shuffle, too high in the mix, obliterating the atmosphere of prowling menace the track attempts to achieve.

Mercifully, Vanian attempts no nu-metal rap, opting to speak the verses in villainous basso profundo, and sing the choruses. Sadly though, the lyrics he has to work with, are not great. The verses attempt a composite picture through a series of discrete images, with our narrator as a shadowy assassin: 'Night gloves, black gown, job done, quit town'. So far, so good, in terms of melodrama and mystique. However, the chorus makes everything a bit too literal, with the narrator claiming that 'We're just having some fun, messing 'round with a gun ... I'm just killing some time, it's a fantasy crime'. Is the narrator actually a killer, or just a fantasist sitting at home playing video games and imagining the real carnage? There's a sense of the band trying to prove they can be as 'edgy' as anything else 2001 has to offer, and it really doesn't suit them.

'Thrill Kill' was Pinch's first Damned songwriting credit: an inauspicious start, for which he would more than make up for in the future. And as for the Captain? Well, it's certainly one of his weaker contributions to the *ouvre*.

'She' (Captain Sensible / David Vanian)

An uptempo firecracker of a track, this gushing tribute from Vanian to his bride-to-be, takes in swampy blues, rockabilly and Doors-ish psychedelia, melding them with lurid Gothic imagery, to great effect. Sensible's picks out a dirty blues riff in E, and the band joins in, Pinch throwing in double-kick flams and spectacular fills. The verses take a call-and-response format: a repeated chant of 'She knows', played off against Vanian's voice with a vintage 1950s tube mic effect, detailing exactly what it is that she knows: ' ... about all the evil in this world ... what blackness lurks in our souls' etc. At the chorus, Vanian's voice morphs from rockabilly twang to Jim Morrison croon, proclaiming: 'She makes me feel like a king.' The middle eight uses Vanian's descriptive powers to vivid effect, as – back in scratchy 1950s mode – he rhapsodises on his subject: 'Eyes limpid pools of passion / Lips of deepest, darkest damson ... like an emissary of sin.' Heady stuff!

The following verse breaks down to vocals and Pinch's acrobatic drums, before an extended out-chorus introduces dramatic choral backing vocals and Sensible's especially frenzied, strangulated lead work. Eventually – as the drums drop to half-time – the tracks softens, Monty's delicate, heartfelt piano transforming this full-blooded rocker into a poignant ballad, concluding with Vanian's velvet tones asserting that, 'She drags my world awake'.

It's a suitably over-the-top tribute to Patricia, reflecting elements of her musical past by combining Gun Club-esque rootsy blues punk with The Sisters of Mercy's gothic glamour: a potentially awkward blend, which The Damned carry off with aplomb.

'Lookin' For Action' (David Vanian / Captain Sensible / Pinch / Patricia Morrison / Laurence Burrow)

The album's only song credited to the entire band, is also probably the closest they've ever come to full-on hardcore punk. Any thought of melody is cast aside, with impact being the sole aim. Pinch's UK82 scene background certainly comes to the fore, as he urges the track along with a relentless 'D-beat': the distinctive pulverising rhythmic gallop that Stoke anarcho-punk legends, Discharge, pioneered, which became so widely used in hardcore that it lent its name to a whole sub-genre. Pinch kicks off with a flabbergasting solo drum intro, acting like a starting pistol, sending the band flying out of the blocks. The main riff is atypical of The Damned, in that it owes nothing to traditional pop or rock 'n' roll conventions, again sounding closer to the proto-thrash metal chord progressions used by the spiky-topped likes of Discharge or GBH.

It must be said that Pinch, Sensible and Morrison sound pretty convincing as a hardcore band (Monty doesn't appear on the track, despite receiving a writing credit under his real name, Laurence Burrow). Pinch is obviously in his element; Morrison steps up admirably, playing with a growling tone and an aggression level heard nowhere else on the record; and Sensible keeps things raw, alternating between pummelling block chording and gnarled lead breaks with admirably reckless abandon. Only Vanian sounds slightly less at ease here, not being given to frantic screaming or macho bellowing you might expect to hear over such a backing. The rich baritone voice so integral to many Damned recordings, has no place here; Vanian opting instead for a transatlantic half-spoken/half-yelled approach, which at least fits the meaningless-but-excitable rock 'n' roll nonsense lyrics: 'Faster, faster, thrill me baby, yeah! / I'm fuelled up and ready / But hey, don't mess with my hair!') Sensible takes a jaw-droppingly impressive double-tracked solo, and then around 2:40 – after another quick verse and chorus – everything descends into a chaotic din, harking back to 'I Feel Alright', concluding the track with a minute and a half of pure noise.

It's not the album's most profound or sophisticated song, but it's pretty invigorating, showing The Damned could play as fast and hard as the new punk breed.

'Would You Be So Hot (If You Weren't Dead?)' (Captain Sensible)

This power-pop gem has a bright, upbeat quality, contrasting with its acidic lyric, which looks at John Lennon's legacy, finding him less a saint than the fawning critical consensus might suggest. 2001 marked the 30th anniversary of Lennon's *Imagine* album, prompting a slew of retrospective articles on the late Beatle, and increased airplay for the album's overplayed title track: all of which seems to have raised the Captain's ire. A guitar riff recalling *Revolver*-era Beatles introduces the song, establishing the chords that underpin the bold, poppy verses. The chorus contrasts, Pinch's rumbling floor-tom rolls and a chromatically-rising bass line ramping up the tension considerably, as the lyric's polemic intensifies.

Each verse attacks Lennon's legacy from a different angle. Verse one questions whether Lennon would be so widely celebrated if his erstwhile collaborator Paul McCartney had been the one assassinated, evoking McCartney's solo-composed 'Yesterday' in the process: 'Suddenly, you are twice the man you used to be ... Would it be different if he had gone instead? Would you be so hot if you weren't dead?' Verse two points out the hypocrisy of Lennon's public pleas for peace and love, while privately he was known to be quite bitter and cruel; and verse three suggests that some of his contemporaries were more talented, and 'Damn the grovelling writers who disregard your flaws'. It's a surprisingly harsh stance, but at least represents a considered viewpoint from a true scholar of classic pop, rather than mere reactionary punk nihilism. The track moves into a half-time instrumental section oscillating between C and F, with Sensible taking a meandering solo, before Monty's piano sneaks in a snatch of 'Imagine' during the closing moments.

This song is unlikely to change the mind of any diehard Lennon fan, but it's a cracking pop song, and certainly the better of Sensible's celebrity musings to appear on the album, as we shall see.

'Absinthe' (David Vanian)

Vanian's first solo composition on *Grave Disorder* oozes the decadence and glamour of a bygone age. 'Absinthe' celebrates the notorious 'green faerie': a drink long beloved of artists, poets and madmen, with our narrator embodying the spirit of this devilish intoxicant. It's a sweeping, lush, mid-tempo track, not dissimilar to 'The Dog' from *Strawberries*: seductive, easy-listening, feeling almost like a cabaret number, albeit a very dark one. An atmospheric synth accompanies an apposite speech sample ('Absinthe is the aphrodisiac of the soul ... '), the track then slipping into gear with Sensible's clean E minor guitar arpeggios. A warbling soprano voice follows, perhaps as a sonic representation of the green faerie? Pinch's tight snare roll brings in the verse, Vanian's warm low vocal tone used to full effect in a performance more Vegas showman than punk shouter, and all the better for it.

The dynamics build steadily. At the middle eight, Pinch's alternating snare triplet bars interrupt, fitting six beats in the space of four, creating a staggering sensation mirroring the lyric's intoxication and disorientation: 'As the evening starts to crawl / Dark shadows on the wall / Are dancing and inviting you to come and taste it all.' Sensible wild fuzz guitar squalls compound the confusion, the band then gliding smoothly into the final chorus, now with added harmonies. A final tag verse delivers the punchline, our narrator telling his victim that, after their night together, 'If you're not completely mad, I'll be your best friend'. Vanian drops to a low E on the final word, ending with a wicked chuckle, and a chromatic piano descent reflecting the insanity that absinthe can bring about.

It's a wonderful, evocative track capturing Vanian at the peak of his powers, and The Damned at their most 'showbiz' – which, once in a while, is no bad thing.

'Amen' (Captain Sensible / Pinch)

Organised religion is revisited here, a subject last broached on 1979's 'Antipope', and it seems that the band's view has not mellowed in the least. Vanian resumes the role of hellfire preacher, urging his congregation into unquestioning obedience while delighting in his own hypocrisy, his stern baritone giving weight and authority to his pulpit proclamations. Tolling church bells introduce the track along with real-life sermonising preachers who will resurface throughout. Vanian delivers his sermon, interspersed with wordless backing vocals, evoking monastic plainsong and concluding every verse with 'Amen'. After verse two, a brief peaceful interlude drops the rhythm to a bass drum pulse with choral harmonies, as the church bells toll. After a thunderous tom-tom pattern, Vanian-as-preacher implores, 'Don't stand there looking sheepish, come and join the flock inside'.

Each verse takes aim at Christianity's more disturbing fringes: with references to burning crosses; a swipe at those who deny scientific truths ('Old Galileo's long forgot / Though he was right and we are not'); and a dig at America's many TV preachers ('A thousand channels, take your pick / Another mystic lunatic'). It's pretty familiar punk subject matter but done well with a healthy blend of sly humour and righteous anger.

After the Captain's blazing wah-wah solo and a final verse, we're back to the heavenly chorus in D, Monty's cathedral organ accompanying Pinch's booming Bo Diddley beat, more lead guitar wailing over the top. US preachers cry out 'Thank you, Jesus!', and the music fades down to organ and chorus, and then to nothing, as the track appears to naturally end. But around 5:20, as an odd postscript, an almost new-age-sounding track fades in: all shimmering keyboards, tastefully echoing guitars and electronic drums, with a background of birdsong and flowing water. It's all rather eerily soothing, especially when a heavily-effected voice chimes in, saying 'You need to do that ... it's so simple ... it's fast, it's free, it's easy'. A truly weird, but certainly interesting and unexpected conclusion to an otherwise hard-driving track.

'Neverland' (Captain Sensible)

The second and less successful of Captain Sensible's 'grumbling about celebrities' songs here, takes a potshot at Michael Jackson, poking fun at his videos and his public persona's more ludicrous aspects, circa 1996, when the song originally appeared on the Captain's solo album, *Mad Cows &*

Englishmen. There are a couple of funny lines, but even Vanian's splendid deadpan delivery can't disguise the impression that the lyrics were hastily cobbled together. The opening lines are a perfect example: 'Michael used to tell us he was bad, bad, bad / And all his funky records made us glad, glad, glad.' There's no way Sensible could've known at the time of its writing, how the words would resonate given the later disturbing Jackson allegations, making the song now feel somewhat frivolous and in poor taste – not that this would necessarily bother the Captain one bit!

Musically, it's punchy pop-punk with a catchy guitar riff. Neither verse nor chorus are especially melodically engaging, but the energetic and exuberant performance is enough to keep the listener interested. In the soft organ-led minor-key middle eight, Vanian croons speculatively about Jackson's marriage to Lisa Marie Presley, then Sensible takes a superb solo before a final chorus and fade-out.

'Neverland' is the *Grave Disorder* track sounding closest to the Brain-James-era band, with Pinch and Sensible in particular evoking 1977's reckless abandon. But the song itself feels slightly dashed off compared to the excellent material surrounding it. If 'Neverland' had cropped up as a B-side, it would've been an unexpected treat, but as an album track, it doesn't quite meet the high standards the band had set themselves for this album.

''Til the End of Time' (Captain Sensible)
A curious composition, feeling like a throwback to the gothic synth-driven (and Captain-less) *Phantasmagoria* era, but with a generous dash of middle-eastern exotica thrown in for good measure. Pinch mostly sits this one out, as a drum unit provides the unchanging rhythm. Instrumentation is mostly kept spare: bass sticking to unobtrusive root notes, with subtle guitar glimmering with chorus and tremolo. Monty does most of the heavy-lifting, coaxing cinematic strings and Lionel Hampton-esque vibraphone lines from his synths.

Musically, the song seems to owe a debt to Maurice Jarre's main title theme to *Lawrence of Arabia* (1962), which in turn owes much to the orientalist works of Russian romantic composers like Borodin and Rimsky-Korsakov (already featured, in tape-loop form, on 'Curtain Call'), and later, Rachmaninoff. There are also hints of the Duke Ellington/Juan Tizol classic, 'Caravan', particularly in the shuffling, off-beat rhythm and use of the Phrygian scale. The two simple sections are hypnotic, repeating with little variation except for Monty's lines harmonising with the vocal melody; that of the verse being taken up as a wordless chant towards the end.

The lyrics, declaring obsessive, doomed passion, are fairly corny on paper but make perfect fodder for Vanian, who has a gift for selling this kind of song. Intimately close-mic'ed, his voice absolutely makes this recording: his sonorous bass tones are a commanding presence despite the gentle delivery; the high notes strong and heartfelt.

It's probably not the most essential Damned song, and certainly not one you'd use to introduce the band to a new listener, but it's an intriguing oddity and a welcome change of mood and tempo.

'Obscene' (David Vanian / Captain Sensible)

The pace picks up sharply with this pointed critique of celebrity culture, which blends Gothic bombast with punk power, to startling effect. A brief keyboard intro and thunderous timpani bring us straight into the chorus and its chant of 'Obscene! The scene! The dream!'. It's an urgent stomp, Monty's nagging organ line only increasing the tension. The verses relax a little, the opening phrase of Vanian's sweeping vocal melody unexpectedly reminiscent of the first line of Anita Baker's soul classic, 'Sweet Love' (1986).

After a second full chorus, the momentum carries over into a pounding middle eight, before plunging back into an extended chorus, Vanian breaking out his falsetto: not heard since 'Plan 9 Channel 7' back in 1979. An unexpected coda has the band run through the chords in a kind of lounge combo jazz waltz, complete with Dave Brubeck-esque piano flourishes – a slightly tongue-in-cheek twist to proceedings.

The lyrics decry the way we elevate celebrities to ridiculous heights – treating them as 'Demi-gods on golden thrones' – yet simultaneously relish their downfall, when their ' ... descent to hell becomes our breakfast thrill'. It's a savage culture, but the allure of immortality remains: 'Flesh and blood may now decay / But forever young, always you will stay.' It's a great track with a real sense of urgency and drama, and at 2:47 in length, doesn't waste a second.

'W' (Pinch / Tom Savage)

The band hadn't taken a pop at a US president since 'Bad Time For Bonzo' in 1982. But here, Pinch and co-writer Tom Savage (a prolific Peterborough-based punk producer, engineer and musician) set their sights on the then recently-elected president, George Walker Bush Jr: often nicknamed 'W', hence the title. Rather than go for the jugular with direct, accusatory lyrics, 'W' takes a more playful, sardonic approach in true Damned style, the lyric framed as an appreciation of Bush minor, proclaiming with sarcastic glee: 'It'll make my day when I see your face on a dollar bill.' Discarding anger and outrage for wit and wordplay, the words allude to the dubious circumstances surrounding Bush's election victory ('They counted you out, then they counted you in and they're counting still'), and refer to his 'puppeteers' (The cadre of more experienced 'advisers' led by Dick Cheney, who many felt held the real power over the rather feckless president) before concluding with 'For all the lies you're about to tell / May the Lord make us truly thankful'. It's a smart, fun send-up, neatly avoiding the pitfalls of punk cliché; set to a fine pop melody, with a backing blending driving mid-tempo punk with electronica.

Apparently, during this era, Pinch's preferred songwriting tool was a PlayStation music game (most likely *Music 2000*), which allowed the console to be used as a synth, sequencer, drum machine and sampler. The first verse has the programmed rhythm and bass line playing a two-chord vamp, with Vanian's vocal and Sensible's guitar the only 'organic' musical ingredients, until the full band crashes in at the chorus. After chorus two, Monty takes a keyboard solo, Sensible punctuating with blasts of wonderfully ugly square-wave distortion. The last chorus is extended, with dual backing vocal lines: one side repeating 'They counted you out'; the other, 'God may forgive us', over which the Captain unleashes some positively incendiary lead guitar before everything concludes on a wholly unexpected D# minor chord.

It's a supremely catchy pop song, which, at over five minutes, doesn't feel overly long. It has also dated surprisingly well: the electronic elements being quirky enough to still sound fun and interesting without seeming jarring, and a lyric that continues to ring true and raise a wry smile.

'Beauty of the Beast' (Laurence Burrow / David Vanian)

The album concludes with this haunting, elegiac tribute to the iconic villains and ghouls of Hollywood's golden age, whose influence on Dave Vanian's stage persona cannot be overstated. The song's writers Vanian and Oxy Moron, are the sole performers here, with keyboards the only accompaniment to Dave's powerful vocal. A late-romantic style piano introduction opens, with booming bass octaves and elaborate Rachmaninoff-like flourishes, settling into a delicate, mournful instrumental verse theme in F minor. Sustained organ chords add to the sorrowful, almost funereal atmosphere. The strings take us to a crescendo, and at 1:50, the vocal finally begins.

The lyrics skilfully set the scene, first in a cinema – where 'Flickering, the shadows fall across my eyes, across the walls' – and then through the screen and into the movie itself, with 'The mists that creep / The hound that howls'. Verse two goes a step further, with a roll call of legends including Bela Lugosi, Boris Karloff, Basil Rathbone, Lon Chaney, Peter Lorre and Vincent Price: 'Now all gone', but still 'Looming pallid on the screen'. The repeating chorus refrain goes to the very heart of Vanian's fascination, posing the question, 'Is it only I can see the beauty of the beast?' As with any of the Damned's Gothic dalliances, there's plenty of melodrama here. But it doesn't detract from what is – beneath it all – a touching and heartfelt tribute to the silver screen's greatest villains and a requiem for a lost era.

So, Who's Paranoid? (2008)

Personnel:
David Vanian: Vocals
Monty Oxymoron: Keyboards
Stuart West: Bass
Pinch: Drums
Captain Sensible: Guitar
Additional personnel:
Bela Emerson: Cello and saw on 'Nature's Dark Passion'
The Brighton Gay Men's Chorus: Vocal harmonies on 'Dr. Woofenstein'
Recorded at The Doghouse, Oxfordshire; Chapel Studios, Lincolnshire; Audio Design, San Diego
Recorded by Adam Whittaker – except for 'Perfect Sunday' and 'Little Miss Disaster' by Ewan Davies; and drums on 'Dr. Woofenstein' by Ben Moore
Mixed by Jim Spencer – except for 'Since I Met You', 'Nature's Dark Passion' and part two of 'Dark Asteroid' by Adam Whittaker; and 'Little Miss Disaster' by Ewan Davies
Record label: The English Channel
Released: November 2008
Highest chart position: uncharted
Running time: 65:59
Current edition: Out of print.

Grave Disorder certainly re-established The Damned as a creative force, setting them apart from the countless reformed 1970s punk acts who were now making a living on the nostalgia circuit. The band continued to be a hugely popular international live draw, the new songs seamlessly slotting into sets, playing to crowds that were a healthy mixture of long term fans and younger listeners who'd discovered punk in the wake of Green Day's 1994 breakthrough. After an unprecedented seven years without a line-up change, Patricia Morrison finally left the band in 2004, for the happy reason that she was due to give birth to her and Vanian's child. After their daughter was born, Morrison decided not to return to the stage, staying on in a management capacity. Pinch's erstwhile English Dogs bandmate, Stu West, replaced Morrison. West, an un-showy shaven-headed gent, may have lacked Morrison's striking stage presence, but he was a superb player; and with he and Pinch having a proven musical chemistry, West slotted right in with barely any interruption to the band's busy touring schedule.

With the band unhappy with Nitro Records' promotional efforts for *Grave Disorder*, a second record for them was not on the cards. With no label, and no particular pressure to deliver an album, The Damned wrote new songs at their leisure, inserting them into live sets as they saw fit, recording some of the fresh material when time and budget permitted. The first of these occasional sessions was for the 'Little Miss Disaster' single: released on the band's own

Lively Arts records in late 2005, backed with a live version of 'Antipope' on the 7', and an additional live 'The History Of The World (Part 1)' on the CD release. The A-side was a bright blast of power-pop, indicating the new material's general direction, and by 2008, there were enough songs for a new album: accumulated from sessions in three different studios over the preceding three years, and with no credited producer. Without record label backing, the band were obliged to go it alone: their own label, The English Channel, releasing *So, Who's Paranoid?* as a digital download in late October, 2008, and on CD a month later. They did what promotion they could, but minus label resources, the album was never in any danger of troubling the charts.

Reviews were reasonably positive, with several accurately noting that the record owed more to the dark pop of *Strawberries* or *Phantasmagoria* than to the early straight-up punk years. As ever, some reviewers failed to overcome their prejudices, with a few castigating the band for not sounding as 'punk' as expected, and others paradoxically complaining that the album was full of 'generic pop-punk blandness' (Cameron Gordon, *Chart Attack*).

The album title (taken from a line in 'Dark Asteroid') and packaging were a comment on the increasing surveillance levels we all find ourselves under in modern society – as discussed in the penultimate track, 'Nothing' – a situation which has only worsened since 2008. The CD front cover was a mirror-like surface, reflecting the listener's face back at them as an answer to the titular question. Open the CD case, and the disc within was a giant staring eyeball, watching from behind the mirror: an unsubtle but effective comment on the increasingly Orwellian circumstances of our day-to-day lives.

As with the controversial *Not of This Earth/I'm Alright Jack & The Beanstalk* album, there was no initial vinyl release. This was rectified two years later with a deluxe double LP on Devil's Jukebox Records: adding three bonus tracks drawn from the same sessions. 'Half Forgotten Memories' is a sultry, minor-key slow-burn, both affecting and effective, although perhaps too drawn-out at six minutes in length. 'Aim To Please' feels like a deliberate throwback to the Brian James era: a lively sub-three-minute rocker with an aggressive, choppy riff, and Vanian giving his best Iggy Pop yowl, making for an enjoyable – if inessential – addition to the record. 'Time' is a very *Nuggets* slice of mid-1960s garage R&B pop, with great warbling organ, hyperactive drums and blown-out fuzz guitar. It's terrific fun but more of a pastiche/homage than a representation of The Damned, which is presumably why it didn't qualify for the main album running order.

With or without the bonus tracks, *So, Who's Paranoid?* is a tremendous album with consistently high songwriting and production standards. It feels more focussed than *Grave Disorder*, with far fewer weak points, despite its lengthy running time; and to this writer at least, represents the band's finest work since *Strawberries*, which makes it especially upsetting that *So, Who's Paranoid?*, as Sensible conceded to *Rolling Stone* magazine: 'Sunk without a trace.' Although it's had various limited-edition reissues, it's now out of print, making it the most difficult Damned album to obtain, with even second-hand CD copies fetching fairly silly money. One can only hope that the band's current label – Spinefarm – make this under-appreciated masterpiece again widely available, as it really deserves to be heard.

'A Nation Fit for Heroes' (Captain Sensible / Martin Newell)

This hard-driving garage-pop gem sets the tone for things to come, with a fine blend of punk energy, classic pop hooks, evocative harmonic structure and world-weary social commentary. For the most part, the album's writing credits return to the egalitarian approach – this song being the sole exception, Sensible having written it in collaboration with Martin Newell, of underrated jangle-poppers, The Cleaners From Venus.

The track opens with Sensible's rather beautiful jazz-like chord sequence, adding a melancholy edge, and giving the chorus an unexpected emotional weight. Sensible's guitar tone – forsaking his usual 'cranked Marshall stack' overdrive for an almost clean Beatles-like jangle – sets up a strong 1960s garage feel. With Vanian's smooth vocal, the overall effect is not dissimilar to The Stranglers' more poppy moments, which is no bad thing.

Verse one takes a dim view of the vapid ambitions of 21st-century Britons, with life becoming a meaningless quest for empty fame or material goods, even as environmental disaster looms: 'A chance to get your face on some real TV / Some petrol and a car so you can feel free.' The chorus clarifies the titular irony, calling for an 'ovation for the Neros, who fiddle while the world's burning down'. The second verse and chorus take a similarly scathing look at the tabloid press – a favourite Sensible target – which is helping turn us into a 'zombie land for zeros'.

The band begin the album sounding – dare I say it – mature; with peerless musicality balancing the righteous anger. It's a good fit for them, even if some critics refuse to accept anything that moves beyond The Damned's early primitive fury.

'Under the Wheels' (The Damned)

After a strong start, things kick up another gear with this bona fide masterpiece: a perfect melding of punk velocity and sweeping gothic drama. Pinch's jackhammer drums soon whip the huge, ominous bass line up to almost hardcore speed, staccato guitar chords increasing the urgency. After the slightly middle-eastern-flavoured intro, the verse instrumentation thins out to the rhythm section only, focussing on Vanian's commanding vocal. In surprisingly poetic terms, our narrator is an innocent soul, helplessly swept along, the relentless modern world corrupting and crushing him: 'Green, sacrifice me / Float down the stream / Over the waterfall, send me.' The floodgates then open into the chorus' rich wall of organ and guitar, Sensible's arpeggios harmonising with the lead vocal. The clamour subsides slightly for the final two chorus lines: 'Under the skin I crawl / But under the wheels I fall.' A hushed, atmospheric middle eight section allows Vanian the opportunity for some spooky whispering, before an intro riff reprise and extended chorus. The almost pastoral outro, with its wash of keyboards, backwards guitar and semi-submerged speech samples, evokes *Dark Side of the Moon*-era Pink Floyd, bringing peace after the preceding four-and-a-half-minute tumult. Both song and performance are passionate, inventive, and every bit the equal of anything in the band's back catalogue.

'Dr. Woofenstein' (The Damned)
A distinct change of tone here takes us in an odd, if enjoyable, new direction. Eerie sound effects support a barely discernible voice whispering, 'Mr President ... Wake up ... This is not a dream', before a ringing alarm clock opens the song proper, diving straight into the chorus.

The music is not what we'd normally expect from The Damned. It proceeds at a stately tempo, sounding surprisingly like late-1960s Beatles: with Ringo-esque tom fills, chiming 'Let It Be' piano chords, round-toned melodic bass, and guitar echoing George Harrison's rosewood Telecaster lines on the likes of 'Don't Let Me Down' (1969). But rather than match this with Beatlesque vocal harmonies, The Damned take the rather more drastic step of adding an honest-to-goodness male voice choir – The Brighton Gay Men's Chorus, to be precise – lending the song a certain pomp and circumstance. The overall effect is reminiscent of producer Bob Ezrin's more bombastic work: like Pink Floyd's *The Wall* (1979); Kiss' wonderful catastrophe of a rock opera, *Music From 'The Elder'* (1981); or much of Alice Cooper's earlier material. There are also hints of *Hunky Dory*-era David Bowie and early Roxy Music: especially in Vanian's suave lounge-lizard minor-key-verse delivery.

A heady mix, then; all the more intriguing through lyrics describing the eponymous doctor's nefarious machinations: 'Hatching shadowy schemes, overthrowing us beings'. It's as if the doctor may be the allegorical counterpart of a real-life villain, but we can only guess who that would be. Luckily, it's entirely possible to enjoy the song without this layer of meaning, and it stands up nicely as perhaps the band's most theatrical number since 'Grimly Fiendish'; although that earlier track's very English music hall pop is a world away from the portentous concept rock of 'Dr Woofenstein'.

'Shallow Diamonds' (The Damned)
Perhaps the most straight-ahead pop song on the album, 'Shallow Diamonds' is catchy almost to a fault, with a simple yet naggingly effective vocal hook that digs into your brain and doesn't let go. We're back to 1960s-inspired power pop here, the tight, lively rhythm section adorned with nothing more elaborate than almost-clean guitar and reedy Farfisa organ: a timeless blend heard in both countless *Nuggets*-era garage bands and the new wave sounds of Elvis Costello and the Attractions etc. Only the intro's filtered programmed drum rhythm gives any hint of the post-1966 musical landscape. The song structure has a similar time-honoured simplicity, alternating between an

A-major verse pattern incorporating the 'diamonds' hook, a chorus in E and a middle eight in F# minor.

The lyrics question the enduring appeal of said precious stones and the madness it can cause. Verse one hits hardest, urgently warning that 'Wars are being fought over diamonds / Lives are sold and bought over shallow diamonds'; the chorus pointing out that all this human suffering is for nothing more than 'compressed carbon ... no more use than a candy bar'. It's a valid point, but things go downhill a little from there with some truly excruciating couplets cropping up: 'Got the magic to make you drool / Make a businessman shaggable,' anyone? No? The middle eight though, is a fun diversion, in which Vanian – drenched in 1950s-style slap echo, gives a nod to Conway Twitty's classic ballad, 'It's Only Make Believe' (1958).

All in all, it's a perfectly serviceable pop song, if feeling slightly 'by the numbers' in places; and the lyrics, though well-intentioned, are rather clumsy. Not bad, but one of the album's weaker moments.

'Since I Met You' (The Damned)

In another twist, the band veer dramatically off the expected path, with what can only be described as a power ballad: albeit one laced with a good deal of postmodern irony. *So, Who's Paranoid?* was a divisive album among Damned fans, with those hoping for a conventionally punk-sounding record, left disappointed; and I imagine this track would've been especially hard for those listeners to swallow. However, I rather like it! It's a tour-de-force for Monty, as he tastefully embellishes the verses with piano and a lush Mellotron flute arrangement ala The Moody Blues' late-1960s/early-1970s heyday. The choruses bring in the rock bombast, in an almost Queen-like fashion.

But it's the wonderfully self-aware lyrics that are really effective: the lovelorn narrator complaining about the effect love songs have on him ('even the stupid ones'), seemingly oblivious to the fact that his narration in itself is an inane love song, complete with endless corny rhymes ('you/new/true/stew' and 'be/see/me/incessantly', for instance). It all works especially well, thanks to Vanian's absolutely straight-faced delivery with nary a hint of a knowing wink, allowing us to enjoy the song on an entirely lush ballad surface level if we wish; or to delight in its deconstruction of genre cliches, if we're feeling a tad more cynical.

'A Danger to Yourself' (The Damned)

The garage-punk influences are back in full-effect on this driving rocker: one of the album's most effective songs. We hit the ground running, Sensible's single guitar keeping a driving rhythm, while interjecting a constant stream of inventive melodic fills. Vocal harmonies elevate the choruses, and the dynamics really don't let up until the middle eight.

The lyrics take a swipe at the foolhardy pastimes of the idle rich, and the myth of the 'gentleman adventurer': poking fun at aristocratic types who – for want of anything useful to do – set out to conquer nature, only to find that nature doesn't wish to be conquered:

> Stuck in the Arctic 'cos you haven't got a clue
> Not short of money, there was nothing else to do
> You're posh, you're stupid and you've got to make your name
> But when disaster strikes, there's no-one else to blame

For the middle eight, Vanian takes on the role of the intrepid blue-blood himself, proclaiming, 'I've gotta make this climb / Hold the front page baby, 'cos I may be some time': echoing the last words of Captain Lawrence Oates, who sacrificed himself trying to save Robert Falcon Scott's ill-fated 1910 Antarctic expedition – an early example of exactly the type of venture this song critiques.

An instrumental section follows, allowing Pinch and West to ease off the gas a little, as Sensible and Monty trade-off improvised passages – their psychedelic roots clearly on display – building to a scored melodic lead guitar section. Sensible sustains the guitar heroics over a final chorus, which halts abruptly at Vanian's yell of 'You're bad for your health!' This concludes a fierce but irresistibly-tuneful track; the band successfully marrying punk's fire, energy and bitter class resentment to the musical vocabulary of their beloved 1960s psych-pop.

'Maid for Pleasure' (The Damned)

Sadomasochism is a subject hinted at in a number of Damned songs: notably the debut album's 'Feel The Pain'. But never before have they broached the topic so directly. The lyric discusses a helpless young woman, forced into a degrading submissive role, with Vanian delivering lines like 'High heels and a pretty bow get the job done nicely / The apron hides a tortured soul as she cleans the place up nightly' with an appropriately lascivious leer. The chorus confirms her unwillingness to participate, stating 'She don't want to see him anymore', but also, intriguingly, 'She don't want to be him anymore'. Verse two brings a twist – worthy of The Kinks' gender-blurring classic, 'Lola' (1970) – revealing the helpless maid to actually be a role-playing businessman: a 'high flyer in a different world', performing chores for his 'lady master', for masochistic thrills.

Some of the album's hardest-driving music accompanies this delightfully sordid tale. Pinch's punishing intro drum pattern (Not dissimilar to Neal Smith's intro to Alice Cooper's 'Billion Dollar Babies' (1973)) goes on to underscore the entire track. Sensible adds a gnarly riff with an almost jazz-like discordant quality, reminiscent of late Black Flag: the L.A. hardcore pioneers who grew from heavily Damned-indebted origins to create their own challenging, intense brand of punk in the early-to-mid 1980s. While many of this album's tracks feature a relatively clean, poppy guitar tone, Sensible's sound here is a full-on heavily overdriven 'Marshall stack turned up to ten' tone, adding to the song's relentless intensity. In the choruses, Monty adds an insistent, nagging piano D-note drone – a nod to John Cale's single-note playing on The Stooges' 'Now I Wanna Be Your Dog' (1969): perhaps punk's ultimate anthem of submissive degradation – and after the final chorus, plays gentle, reflective chords – the calm after the restless, turbulent storm of the song gone before.

'Perfect Sunday' (The Damned)
The band really bring out the fireworks for this introduction. It's a magnificent opening, recalling The Who at their stadium-slaying peak. Unfortunately, the ensuing track is a little underwhelming in comparison. It certainly drives along nicely, with a mean and moody lead vocal, but the whole thing hangs on a riff both naggingly familiar and a bit basic.

The lyrics are an exercise in nostalgia-skewering, evoking images of a cosy, idealised British Sunday that never really existed in the verses, negating them with the chorus: 'Perfect Sunday past, moving on.' This cynical view of suburban aspirations echoes The Monkees' 'Pleasant Valley Sunday' (1967). But 'Perfect Sunday' lacks the focus or impact of Goffin and King's pop gem, with both lyric and music feeling workmanlike, rather than inspired. Things get more interesting around 3:10, when the track morphs into a more relaxed drum pattern with Townshend-esque acoustic guitars. The chorus builds to a final crescendo featuring some full-throated ad-libbing from Vanian. It's an impressive coda, which almost makes up for the slightly perfunctory feel overall.

'Nature's Dark Passion' (The Damned)
If 'Since I Met You' felt like a showcase for the talent of Monty and Dave, 'Nature's Dark Passion' is even more so. The only two band members featuring on the track, they have created a cinematic mini-epic, with Oxymoron crafting a magnificent score, seamlessly blending organic instruments (including Bela Emerson's cello and musical saw) with electronic elements, and Vanian delivering what is arguably a career-best vocal performance.

With lyrics comparing emotions to 'The majestic force of a tidal wave' – shot through with references like 'demonic poison' and 'chaos and madness' – the song is the album's purest representation of the band's gothic side; and yet it's by no means 'goth' music, owing far less to the likes of Bauhaus or Alien Sex Fiend than it does to Belgian chanteur, Jacques Brel. The yearning minor-key melody and air of existential angst are very Brel-like, and Vanian steps into the role of tortured cabaret artiste with aplomb, giving a wonderfully nuanced performance showing beautifully controlled dynamics and phrasing. Again, those looking for punk rock will be disappointed. But the wonderful thing, is that in the midst of what is essentially a hard-pop album, the band can do something like this and make it sound utterly convincing.

'Little Miss Disaster' (The Damned)
Originally released as a standalone single in 2005, 'Little Miss Disaster' is a
happy addition to the album. Its hook-laden pop-punk attack fits in beautifully,
giving the album's second half a real energy jolt. But the intro rather sneakily
wrong-foots us; the urgent throbbing rhythm, increasingly dissonant guitar
chords and spooky synths come to a crescendo, releasing the tension into the
gloriously catchy chorus E major riff.

Vanian's vocal is warm and relaxed, painting a portrait of the title character's
chaotic life with affectionate concern rather than disapproval. After a brief,
positively pretty middle eight with Mellotron flutes underscoring Vanian's
gentle voice, the pace picks back up for a typically magnificent guitar solo from
the Captain.

The protagonist is portrayed as intelligent-yet-reckless, careening through a
life fraught with barroom brawls and abusive men. The final verse concludes by
asking, 'Could it be this special girl lives on, happy ever after?'. The song doesn't
set any new standards for 21st-century feminism, but it is a fitting tribute to the
band's female fans, and the many fierce and brilliant women in punk.

'Just Hangin'' (The Damned)
Railing against the royal family has been a punk staple since the Pistols did
their best to upset the Queen's silver jubilee back in 1977. But it's a trope The
Damned had not contributed to until now. Starting late with the royal-bashing,
they really put the boot in here: taking pot shots at the monarchy institution
as a whole, and individual family members – the verses directly addressing
them, stressing their irrelevance and urging them to abdicate; while the chorus
compares the family's public life to bad TV melodrama, and suggests a rather
drastic remedy: 'It's a lousy soap, and they've got no hope / Somebody get a
rope, just hangin'.' Yikes! I don't imagine the band are seriously advocating the
lynching of the Windsor clan, but it makes for a striking statement.

With such an aggressive lyric, we might expect equally fearsome music.
The track is fairly up-tempo and reasonably punchy but sadly lacking in the
harmonic interest and melodic muscle so clearly evident elsewhere on the
album. The whole thing is based on two fairly generic chord patterns with little
else happening. The final chorus leads to a slightly underwhelming conclusion.
Don't get me wrong; it's very listenable, with fine performances throughout,
but it doesn't measure up to the best songs here, and I wonder if the album
would've suffered at all, had this track ended up on the proverbial cutting
room floor.

'Nothing' (The Damned)
The album gets back on track immediately with this absolute barnstormer: a
blend of Motorhead-like breakneck rock 'n' roll, and brooding melody harking
pleasingly back to *Machine Gun Etiquette*'s thrashier moments, or 'Therapy'
from *The Black Album*.

111

'Nothing' offers a bleak view of a dehumanising, paranoia-haunted existence in an invasive surveillance state. It begins at a frantic pace, with West's wandering walking bass and Sensible's harsh and discordant lead line (that *diabolus in musica* tritone interval again) almost sounding like a warning alarm. The verse' pummelling back-to-punk-basics B riff brings Vanian in with an angry rasp rarely heard since the early days. The pace sustains into the chorus, with a key change to a mournful B minor, Vanian's vocal becoming darkly melodic – sung rather than snarled – as he states, despairingly: 'Nothing will ever change it ... The lunatics now run the madhouse'.

An instrumental section with a half-time feel brings the Captain's backwards-masked guitar solo, in a welcome hint of *Black Album*-era psychedelic experimentation. The lyrics paint an ever-more unsettling picture of the constant snooping and information-gathering of governments and corporations alike, which leaves us 'Tippy-toeing through the ID age / Like a monkey in a global cage'.

It's a fantastic recording, showing that not only can The Damned still play 'punk' (as defined by a narrow set of stylistic conventions) better than most when they choose, but they can still do so in a unique and inimitable way.

'Dark Asteroid' (The Damned)

Being one of the first punk bands to challenge the genre's conventions of brevity and minimalism, The Damned are no strangers to making tracks boldly reaching beyond the three-minute mark. But here, they really plunge into the unknown, with their most lengthy and ambitious undertaking since 1980's monumental 'Curtain Call'. However, while 'Curtain Call's several movements were seamlessly linked through recurring themes and musical motifs, 'Dark Asteroid' is structurally far simpler, consisting of just two distinct sections: a mid-tempo psychedelic pop song – paying tribute to Pink Floyd's troubled genius, Syd Barrett – and a driving, droning instrumental jam veering towards space-rock and Krautrock.

The vocal section deliberately and affectionately evokes early-Floyd, opening with Monty's trippy Leslie-speaker organ, as Sensible mimics Barrett's distinctive slashing, slippery slide guitar style (as heard on the likes of 'Astronomy Domine' (1967)). Even Vanian can't resist adding a Barrett-like lilt to his verse delivery, sounding briefly like a fey psychedelic waif, although the customary rich croon returns in full force for the choruses.

This deliberate stylistic section demarcation reflects the lyrics. The verses celebrate Syd's life, in a string of Barrett-like wordplay and disjointed images, with particular reference to the infamous Games For May concert: the Floyd's psychedelic extravaganza of 12 May 1967, which included an experimental quadraphonic sound system sending 'Fuzztone echoing through the hall / Screaming and spiralling up the wall', while a stagehand posing as an admiral, handed out flowers to the audience, to 'change the war divisions into a love parade'. In contrast, the tension-building choruses take a dim view of Pink

Floyd's post-Syd existence, accusing them of becoming, 'A corporate brand / Boring and bland / Throw in your hand'. As the final chorus concludes with the question 'So, who's paranoid?', the music fades to complete silence for a second or two. Then just as we're convinced the song is over, the second section begins.

Still in the key of A but at a much swifter tempo, the rhythm section establishes a groove and sticks with it unwaveringly. Sensible and Oxymoron indulge in expansive improvisation, the Captain's wah-wah guitar squalling with a fervent intensity recalling both Jimi Hendrix and the free-jazz saxophone of Albert Ayler or Archie Shepp; while Monty whips up a Hammond storm, overlaying sinister Bernard Herrmann-esque Mellotron strings.

It's an intense, mesmerising performance, drawing not only on Pink Floyd's early expansive freak-outs, such as 'Interstellar Overdrive' (1967), but also Hawkwind – the space-rock pioneers who provided an early home for future Damned associate, Lemmy – and experimental German drone-rockers, Neu!. Granted, it's not necessarily a track you'd listen to every day, but if you're in the right mood, it's a bold and impressive piece of work, supplying a suitably grand conclusion for a fantastic and cruelly-overlooked album.

Evil Spirits (2018)

Personnel:
David Vanian: Vocal
Captain Sensible: Guitar
Paul Gray: Bass
Monty Oxymoron: Keyboards
Pinch: Drums
Additional personnel:
Chris Coull: Trumpet
Kristeen Young: Backing vocals
Tony Visconti: Backing vocals
Recorded at Atomic Sound, Brooklyn, New York
Produced by Tony Visconti
Record label: Search And Destroy, Spinefarm
Released: April 2018
Highest chart position: UK: 7
Running time: 41:06

With *So, Who's Paranoid?* failing to make much of a splash, and without a record label to demand a follow-up, there was no pressure to create new music post-2008. The Damned's excellent live shows were still a hugely popular draw, and it would've been the easiest thing in the world for them to simply trade on their considerable legacy, rehashing the old hits to satisfy the endless public demand for nostalgia. However, while their sets would always, understandably, be drawn largely from their impressive back catalogue, with four strong songwriters in the line-up, the band's creative spirit would not be quelled for long. Also, unlike some of their more celebrated peers, The Damned's perennial outsider status in UK punk – constantly overlooked and underestimated by critics and pop historians alike – had left them with a collective chip on their shoulder and a constant need to carry on, prove themselves and succeed against the odds.

In order to accomplish this lofty goal, they enlisted the services of legendary Marc Bolan and David Bowie producer Tony Visconti, whose work on the thin white duke's final project, *Blackstar* (2016), convinced Vanian that Visconti had the vision and aesthetic The Damned were looking for. Legendary producers don't come cheap, so the band turned to their fans. One successful crowdfunding campaign later, they were able to book two weeks in Visconti's New York studio, commencing in November 2017.

With the recording sessions booked, all four songwriters got to work, with Vanian, in particular, contributing more enthusiastically than he had to the largely Sensible-led *So, Who's Paranoid?*. The band amassed a list of 20 or 22 new songs (the Captain's recollection varies slightly from the official website account), from which Visconti chose a lean ten to record.

Obviously, it wouldn't be The Damned if everything went totally according to plan, and this time the fly in the ointment was bassist Stu West's sudden – if amicable – departure, just before recording commenced. Fortunately, Paul Gray had kept in touch with the band over the years – collaborating with the Captain in the wonderfully named Sensible Gray Hairs – and was able to save the day, stepping in at the eleventh hour. Initially announced as a temporary guest, Gray has stayed on, and with Barrie Masters' sad passing preventing further Eddie and the Hot Rods reunions, looks likely to remain, which is excellent news for fans of the *Black Album/Strawberries*-era band.

Rather than overdubbing individual performances, Visconti preferred to record the band playing together, capturing a genuine group dynamic: an old-school approach which suited The Damned perfectly, recalling their initial sessions with Nick Lowe all those years ago. With only two weeks to record the album, the schedule was tight. But the band and Visconti worked well together, Vanian in particular clicking with the producer. The Captain's only grumble, as he told *Louder Than War* magazine, was that 'I feel there could have been raunchier guitar work on the album. He wasn't really into loud guitars and noodling and kept a lid on all that sort of thing'. While Visconti may have curbed Sensible's wilder indulgences, he also helped deliver the band's tightest, most focussed set of songs since the early-1980s: tracks that married punk's fire and energy to 1960s baroque pop's melodious darkness and drama, creating a sound that was recognisably 'classic' without feeling dated or tied to a specific past era.

For once, the critics agreed, with *Evil Spirits* garnering more attention than the last several releases, and receiving possibly the most consistently positive reviews of any Damned album. Of course, some writers still seemed to almost wilfully miss the point – complaining that the album was somehow not 'punk' enough and far-removed from the raw 'New Rose' sound – apparently unaware of the band's 40-year evolution and unable to recognise the punk urgency and political fury that drove much of the record. Nevertheless, *Evil Spirits* was an inarguable triumph, delighting long-term fans, winning back those whose attention had wandered, and attracting swathes of new listeners. It climbed to number 7 in the UK, making it the band's highest-charting album to date.

Part of this success can be credited to the label's effective promotion strategy. London-based emo imprint, Search And Destroy, and Finnish extreme metal label, Spinefarm, may have seemed like an odd fit for a group of UK punk veterans. But with Spinefarm's distribution via major label Universal, they were able to ensure that people were aware of the album, which can be a challenge in today's fraught music industry.

The album was beautifully packaged, with Laurence and Mitchell Thomas' cover pastiche of vintage film noir posters evoking the classic Hollywood style and glamour so beloved of Dave Vanian; while also hinting towards the music's darkness and excitement.

'Standing on the Edge of Tomorrow' (David Vanian)

The first album in a decade demanded a bold opening, and this sweeping sci-fi epic delivers spectacularly. It conveys an urgent ecological message wrapped in a retro-futurist space opera, juxtaposing kitschy vintage and ultra-modern sounds. The lyrics bring a stark realism, addressing the current environmental crisis, with the warning, 'This time could be the last time / Maybe the only time to get it right', over the band's urgent A-minor chug.

But the song soon leaves the realm of the factual, moving to a boldly melodic bridge recalling the dramatic orchestral pop of Scott Walker or Barry Ryan. Vanian speculates that mankind may have to abandon Earth altogether and seek a new home among the stars: 'Gravity won't hold us down / Our journey's begun, we tear through the clouds.' At the chorus, over booming timpani and portentous choral harmonies, Vanian emphasises humankind's precarious situation: poised on the cusp of either drastic action or catastrophe.

The band are in fine form, and Vanian's vocals – here and throughout the album – are exemplary: powerful, nuanced, and with a hint of showbiz flair. After the final chorus, Sensible is let off the leash, letting rip with a full-throated solo, while a horn section sounds a heroic, almost Wagnerian motif, as the track fades into the distance like the ship carrying mankind into the vast, dark unknown. It's a compelling dark fantasy, which works as escapist entertainment, but has a serious message at its core.

'Devil in Disguise' (Pinch / Pat Beers)
The album's most direct rock track – co-written with Pat Beers of Californian retro-garage act, the Schizophonics, wastes no time, crashing straight in with crunching power chords over a tense, syncopated drum rhythm. Vanian affects a gravelly blues growl recalling *L.A. Woman*-era Jim Morrison. Verse two adopts a more regular driving rhythm, sounding not unlike The Ramones' bluesier, less poppy late-1980s sound. The chorus is smoother and more mysterious: Monty's Ray Manzarek-like keyboards coming to the fore, and Sensible trading blasting chords for ringing arpeggios, as Vanian croons the haunting minor-key melody. A burst of heavy 'Itchycoo Park' phasing returns us to the verse.

The lyrics take the point of view of an unnamed right-wing populist politician, and Vanian plays the villain every bit as well as you'd expect: his tone shifting seamlessly from snarling menace to charming suavity with the slickness of a career politician; Vanian also makes some impressive octave leaps here, confirming his voice was perhaps in its finest ever shape. For all that Sensible complained of the absence of 'big guitars' on the album, he was given free reign here, giving a fiery performance, which – combined with Gray's spectacular bass-playing – ensures that the band's rock 'n' roll credentials are fully intact.

'We're So Nice' (Captain Sensible)
'We're So Nice' revisits the Motown-tinged mod-pop sound last heard on 1982's 'Stranger On The Town'. A sunny facade conceals a barbed message mirroring the duplicity of the political figures it targets: familiar types – from the post-Blair British political era – who present an image of reasonable,

affable, centrist moderation, with hawkish, warlike tendencies lurking just below the surface; the right-wing press influence never far away.

Opening with a great raga-tinged string-bending guitar riff in E, the track soon becomes an amped-up stomping Holland/Dozier/Holland Motown rhythm, Gray's growling Rickenbacker bass sounding like a cross between James Jameson and John Entwistle. The verse has a tight groove, with Vanian sounding especially fresh-faced; the bright, poppy melody echoing the narrator's cheerily-diplomatic (on the surface) pronouncements: 'Around the world, when it counts / We've got so much to share, don't we? / We're so nice!' Lush Mellotron strings emphasise the 'niceness', creating a cosy warmth quite at odds with the seemingly-bland lyric's militaristic subtext. A beautifully-harmonised bridge spells out the narrator's true intentions: 'It takes a lot to make a nation want to fight / But you can trust the daily news to put us right / To point us where to go and who has got to die, on a lie.' This is likely to ring some bells for those who remember the beginning of the second Gulf war.

As the track breaks down into cocktail party ambience, Sensible adds stinging lead guitar lines as an acidic contrast to the friendly surface. It's a tremendously catchy slice of power pop, delivering a powerful lyrical sucker punch.

'Look Left' (Pinch / Jon Priestley)

A second contribution from Pinch, this time co-written with current Godfathers bassist Jon Priestley. For a musician who made his name playing some of the harshest anarcho-thrash imaginable, the range and subtlety of Pinch's songwriting is surprising; and of all the songs he's brought to the table, 'Look Left' is probably both the finest, and the furthest-removed from its author's hardcore roots.

It examines the troubling 'post-truth' age in which we live, where the general populace are distracted into apathy or hoodwinked into misdirected rage. It's a theme that could easily turn into a by-the-numbers punk rant. Instead, the tone is wistful and almost elegiac. Rather than a one-dimensional screed, it's a poetic plea for sanity, in a world that's lost touch with the truth. These thoughtful lyrics are set to a stately, tastefully orchestrated ballad with a huge, soaring melodic chorus, once again channelling great 1960s balladeers like The Walker Brothers or The Righteous Brothers. Pinch told *Louder Sound* : 'Tough subject matter is easier to digest when coated in honey rather than vinegar, and the message in this song is so important, I couldn't risk it being a throwaway aggro punk tune that was immediately overlooked'. He certainly succeeded in creating a more substantial vehicle for his message, which carries far more emotional weight in this form than it ever could as a two-minute thrash.

The gentle opening verse, builds to an expansive chorus. Vanian really sells the song's plea to humanity: 'Let's unmask the charade, our time in the shade has overrun/Though dying blooms evade the sun, I'll wait for you'. After chorus two, the instruments fall away, and Vanian sings the repeated refrain: 'While everybody's looking left, what the hell is happening right?': his voice panning across the stereo spectrum accordingly. After a final chorus, Monty's fine Hammond solo builds from simple, smooth melodic lines, to a rhythmic crescendo; Gray in support with some upper-fret melodic bass work.

Recognising the track's potential for mainstream crossover, the band released 'Look Left' as a single, along with a fine promo video. Sadly, the song didn't receive a great deal of radio support. Nevertheless, it's a notable standout, showing further proof of the band's ability to convey a powerful point without preaching or sloganeering.

'Evil Spirits' (Captain Sensible)
Sensible's wish for big guitars was granted on this enjoyably moody 1970s rock jam, which continues the album's political theme while providing a launchpad for some wild instrumental improvisation. The song depicts a tribe who hope a new chief can banish the malevolent spirit plaguing them, only to find that a change of leader doesn't necessarily improve the situation: 'It feels like nothing's changed / Just colours rearranged / Yeah, there must be something going on.' The message is once again akin to that of The Who's 'Won't Get Fooled Again'(1971), and while 'Meet the new boss, same as the old boss' may not be a novel sentiment, it's one that bears repeating.

This track – a hard-driving blues rock groove in A, with latin-tinged syncopation – is the first time The Damned have ventured so far into 'classic rock' territory since the ill-fated *Not of This Earth* album, and it's comforting that they're capable of doing so without resorting to the lumpen cliches that plagued that record. There's nothing especially original about 'Evil Spirits', but the tremendous ensemble performance really elevates the song. It builds from a threatening simmer to a full-on frenzy, by way of an instrumental section recalling Latino rockers, Santana. Vanian gives a commanding performance, and as the track nears its end, Pinch and Monty's inspired interplay, pushes them to greater and greater feats of rhythmic dexterity. Possibly not the most essential track on the record, but an atmospheric and rocking conclusion to side one of the LP, nevertheless.

'Shadow Evocation' (David Vanian / Monty Oxymoron)
This is perhaps the closest thing on this album to the windswept, gothic tone of *Phantasmagoria*, albeit with far less jarring production. Vanian and Oxymoron work brilliantly together, spurring one another to ever more dramatic heights. It begins with a mournful, funereal keyboard theme in B minor, over which disembodied, echoing voices repeat the phrase, 'Faster ... than ever before'.

Over Pinch's galloping drums, a timpani thunderclap heralds Vanian's lead vocal – doubled an octave lower, for a weighty, doom-laden effect that's appropriate given that the lyrics paint a portrait of a haunted individual,

118

fervently pursuing his dream, even as time threatens to catch up with him: 'Am I chasing ghosts / Ghosts of the past in my head? / I tear into the night / Blurring the lines, the lines of my life.' Everything is left vague enough for the listener to apply their own interpretation, but it's hard not to see Vanian himself in the song: still passionately chasing his muse at an age when others might retire and settle down. It's heartfelt and genuinely moving, and the tempestuous soundscape serves to heighten the emotive impact.

Sensible, for once, holds back, keeping to a simple, clean rhythm track. This leaves plenty of room for big chorus vocal arrangements echoing the intro's spoken phrase; Gray's ever-inventive bass rumble; and Monty's liberal dashes of Rachmaninoff piano romanticism. It's both a wonderfully atmospheric pop record and a rare piece of existential introspection from a band who clearly have no intention of going gentle into that good night.

'Sonar Deceit' (Captain Sensible)
A Motown spy-movie theme about the plight of whales, misled by submarine navigation systems, is an unlikely concoction to say the least – and on paper, doesn't sound especially appealing. However, in the hands of Captain Sensible (who else?), these disparate elements coalesce into one of the album's standout pop moments. The 'spy movie' element comes from Sensible's distinctly 'James Bond' lead tone – appropriate, considering Bond, as a Naval commander, was likely responsible for his fair share of 'sonar deceit' – and the chord structure with its frequent unexpected, dramatic changes, echoing the work of long-time Bond composer, John Barry.

Meanwhile, the rhythm section supplies the Motown element, playing a cranked-up version of the uptempo shuffle famously heard on The Supremes' 'You Can't Hurry Love' (1966), and borrowed for Iggy Pop's 1977 classic, 'Lust For Life'. Pinch and Gray add muscle, but retain that authentic 1960s feel, right down to the tambourine accentuating the backbeat. Monty's Farfisa organ and Chris Coull's one-man horn section, bolster the classic soul vibe, skilfully bridging the style gap, mixing filmic sustained melodic lines with snappy Detroit-style riffs.

For me, the lyrics fall into a similar category to the *So, Who's Paranoid?* track, 'Shallow Diamonds', in that they make a perfectly valid point, but out of context, sound a wee bit daft. There's no questioning the Captain's concern for animal welfare, nor his anger at humanity's thoughtless cruelty, but lines like 'A city river's not ideal for ocean dwellers / What makes a fish desert the sea? / Is something there?' have an artlessness that's jarring if you focus too closely. Luckily, Vanian's utterly sincere performance works its charm, and the overall effect is really quite compelling. Add in some big vocal harmonies, plus the ethereal soprano of session singer and frequent Visconti collaborator, Kristeen Young, and you have a cracking pop track that successfully overcomes its own oddness, and would've been a very solid candidate for a single.

'Procrastination' (Monty Oxymoron / Captain Sensible)

The Captain and Monty here join forces to present a quirky, new-wave art-pop gem of a type not really heard from The Damned since the excellent 'Some Girls Are Ugly', which surfaced on the 1986 outtakes and rarities collection, *Damned but Not Forgotten*. Rather than coming out in typical all-guns-blazing style, the track slinks along nicely in its own idiosyncratic fashion, powered by Pinch's slightly off-kilter drum pattern and Gray's slippery bass line; Monty adding trebly garage band Farfisa. For the verses, Vanian reins in his usual dynamic, expressive style, opting for a more relaxed, almost conversational approach, as he expounds on his ability to put off until tomorrow what ought to be done today: 'I'd have done it all by now, but there's something in the way / I'll consult a horoscope just to pick a perfect day.' In the brief bridge, Vanian sings, 'It takes a lifetime to complete my procrastination', suggesting that putting off action has become an all-consuming project in itself.

In a sense, 'Procrastination' feels like a direct counterpoint to 'Shadow Evocation'; the former taking a light tone as it ruefully acknowledges its narrator's procrastination; while the latter stresses the imperative need to act while there is still time – which perhaps tells us something about Vanain and Sensible's relative values.

Released as a digital download in advance of the album, 'Procrastination' met with a mixed reaction from fans: many of whom were clearly hoping for something more representative of the established 'Damned style'. But taken on its own merits, it's a fine pop song, with an easy-going humour that's welcome on an album otherwise quite dark and angry in tone.

'Daily Liar' (David Vanian / Captain Sensible)

Over the years, The Damned, like many other punk bands, have taken plenty of shots at the tabloid press' deception and manipulation. And with the recent political climate and the decline of the notion of objective truth, it's still a depressingly relevant topic.

This new entry into the anti-tabloid canon begins in a stately fashion, with Sensible layering guitar lines in a manner reminiscent of Queen's Brian May, over which Chris Couill adds a bright trumpet fanfare. From this, a 12-string guitar riff emerges, proudly wearing its obvious paraphrase of The Monkees' 'Last Train To Clarkesville' (1966). The manufactured 1960s pop act were a formative influence on many early punks, as Monkees covers by everyone from Sex Pistols to Minor Threat and beyond, will attest to.

Vanian plays the role of the naive everyman, overwhelmed by the sheer volume of information available to him, and 'Drowning in a sea of words', imploring the titular newspaper to provide easy answers and 'Direct me so I can find my way through the obstacles ahead'. As if the Monkees tribute wasn't clear enough, the chorus vocal harmonies and the way the arrangement breaks down to a lone guitar following the chorus, are also cribbed from 'Last Train To Clarksville'; but they veer away from the Monkees template before the track becomes a complete pastiche.

Here the song takes on a looser, more improvisational feel. After an instrumental jam, Vanian's vocal reappears, having shed its previous lighter pop tone, now morphed into the gravel-throated hellfire preacher we've encountered on earlier Damned records. Like a minister sermonising about a sinner's descent to hell, he hollers, 'I'm drowning in a raging sea of words/ Try to hold onto a sentence here and there', working himself into a righteous frenzy as the backing vocal congregation chants 'No no no no no!' with gospel-like fervour. Eventually, an intro fanfare reprise breaks the tension, and we're into the final verse, where our narrator has apparently seen the light: 'Knowing what's right and what is wrong / Your hold on me is gone.' As the final chorus' massed vocal harmonies fade, a mock BBC news bulletin has a plummy-voiced announcer report that 'The human race seems to have lost its mojo', followed by a guffaw of laughter – a fitting conclusion to this playful-yet-pointed piece of protest pop (if you'll pardon the alliteration).

'I Don't Care' (David Vanian)

Concluding the album is Vanian's mini-masterpiece, which somehow manages to feel positively epic, despite its modest 3:17 running time, and lyrics almost as minimal as those of the Ramones' 1977 song of the same title ('I don't care / I don't care about this world / I don't care about that girl', and repeat ...)

Foregoing a traditional verse/chorus structure, the song divides into three distinct movements. The first is a mournful B minor ballad, Monty's lyrical piano accompanying Vanian's expressive baritone, tasteful strings adding to the melancholic ambience as the section progresses. Eventually, the voice drops to a whisper, the piano pauses, and a thundering timpani swell ushers in a fearsome new movement, Pinch's muscular drums and Sensible's clanging, cavernous guitar turning the atmosphere from sorrow to fury. Visconti pulls out all the production stops: a phrase from Coull's overdubbed virtual horn section answers Vanian's declaration of 'I don't care'; a wall of choral harmonies behind. The Captain's richly overdriven D-major chord announces the final movement, the urgent tempo relaxing, and the dark, minor-key tonality giving way to an enigmatic sequence featuring duelling trumpets. The track winds to a gentle halt on a C/D chord, creating a sensation of incomplete resolution.

The lyrics are sparse, mainly consisting of the title repeated over and over, Vanian's delivery tasked with instilling any deeper meaning. However, two brief 'verses' bring a little more clarity. In the opening movement, our narrator muses: 'If the sun would shine, would I change my mind? / No I don't think that'll happen at all'; and as the central movement rages, he elaborates: 'Well, you asked so many questions and you told so many lies / I guess I've had enough, I've come to realise...' The lyric avoids referring to specific world events, but as it's on an album directly addressing the world's turbulent political situation in the era of 'alternative facts' and 'fake news', it's tempting to read it as a comment on this toxic climate's fatigue, despair and apathy. It's a bleak but impactful conclusion to a record showcasing a band who – 42 years into their career – sound as fierce and potent as ever.

Damned collections, Live albums and More

The Damned's chequered recording history – with the band jumping from label to label, their music rights owned by a number of different companies, all keen to cash in on their piece of the legacy – has resulted in a sprawling, messy discography. Each of the band's labels has released their own supposed 'best of' collection, often reconfiguring the same material into multiple – apparently different – issues; with discogs.com currently listing a whopping 48 Damned compilations, several of which misleadingly claim to be the 'definitive anthology'. Additionally, many live recordings have been issued: some well recorded and packaged, released with the band's full consent; and some more shoddy in quality and presentation, although potentially of historical interest. This chapter by no means attempts to definitively cover all of these releases, but should hopefully help the interested listener separate the wheat from the chaff.

Looking at compilations first, *Another Great Record From the Damned: The Best of the Damned* (Ace Records, 1981) was the first 'greatest hits' type package: a fine, but slightly odd mix, combining tracks from *Damned Damned Damned, Machine Gun Etiquette* and *The Black Album* with a couple of single tracks, and the non-Damned track, 'Jet Boy Jet Girl', by Captain Sensible and The Softies. *The Light at the End of the Tunnel* (MCA, 1987) impressively managed to overcome rights issues, for the first time bringing together material from all of the band's different labels, although the inclusion of several inferior remixes caused some confusion.

For those seeking a comprehensive overview of the band's career to date, the best option is definitely *Black Is the Night: The Definitive Anthology* (BMG, 2019). This is the only compilation covering the band's entire career, although it can hardly claim to be 'definitive', as it contains no tracks from either *Not of This Earth* (understandable) or *So, Who's Paranoid?* (unforgivable)! It also focuses heavily on album tracks, ignoring some classic single-only releases. Still, it's a pretty great collection, and an ideal companion for anyone unsure where to start in investigating the band.

All Damned albums from the 1976-1986 period have at some point been reissued in deluxe, expanded editions, helping gather together all of the additional single A and B-sides. But if you have the standard vinyl or single-CD albums and want the rest of the discography without buying a stack of 45s, there are a few compilations to help you on your way; although, annoyingly, not yet a complete and definitive singles and B-sides collection; plus a handful of tracks have never been compiled. *The Chiswick Singles ... and Another Thing* (Chiswick, 2011), is a good place to start. It gathers all the *Machine Gun Etiquette* and *Black Album* A and B sides, along with the fantastic *Friday the 13th EP* and some contemporary odds and ends. *Damned but Not Forgotten* (Dojo, 1985) – known to some fans as 'The Pink Album' – is another fine collection, compiling 'Lovely Money', the alternative single version of 'Dozen Girls', and other *Strawberries*-era B-sides, along with excellent outtakes and alternative versions of tracks from the same era.

The MCA Singles: A's + B's (Connoisseur Collection, 1992) is worth having for the excellent *Phantasmagoria*-era B-sides, although it also highlights the band's increasing reliance on remixes, as MCA's insatiable demand for product, outstripped their creative energy. *Skip off School To See the Damned* (Demon, 1992) collects the Stiff-era 45s, including the heroic ransacking of 'Help', and the Shel Talmy-produced 'Stretcher Case Baby'/'Sick Of Being Sick' single. The Damned's radio sessions are also well worth a listen, with some songs quite different from the familiar versions. There have been a couple of John Peel session compilations, the most comprehensive being *Sessions of the Damned* (Strange Fruit, 1993), which includes the final 1980s recordings with Captain Sensible, bridging the gap between *Strawberries* and *Phantasmagoria*.

While some bands have one great live album that absolutely defines them, The Damned have a plethora of them. None are strictly essential, but many are worth investigating. For an insight into the band's origins, you can't go far wrong with *Live at the 100 Club 6/7/76* (Castle, 2007), which first appeared as an extra disc in the expanded anniversary edition of *Damned Damned Damned*, and was later reissued as an LP in its own right. An ultra lo-fi but fascinating document, it captures the raw power of the band's first-ever gig. *Not the Captain's Birthday Party?* (Demon, 1986) is shoddily packaged, claiming to be an original line-up recording, and listing 'I Fall' as 'I'm Bored'. However, the 27 November 1977 recording date tells us this is actually the post-*Music for Pleasure* line-up, with Lu Edmonds on (largely-inaudible) second guitar and Jon Moss on drums. There are some sound issues, with bursts of horrible screeching microphone feedback, but it's still cool to hear this short-lived version of the band, in action.

Sadly there are no official releases of the Algy Ward line-up, but the Paul Gray years are well covered, with *Live Shepperton 1980* (Big Beat, 1982) offering an extended version of the *Machine Gun Etiquette*-heavy set that made up side four of *The Black Album*. *Mindless, Directionless Energy – Live at the Lyceum, 1981* (ID Records, 1987) showcases a more varied set, including a puerile stumble through The Sweet's 'Ballroom Blitz'; and *Live in Newcastle* (Damned Records, 1983) includes material from *Strawberries* and *Friday the 13th*, along with some priceless stage banter from Sensible!

The increased professionalism of the Captain-less 1985 line-up can be heard on *Fiendish Shadows* (Cleopatra, 1997): a fine set recorded at the Woolwich Coronet in July that year, with a good mix of material including some interesting covers. *Final Damnation* (Restless/Essential, 1989) is an excellent document of the 1988 shows, featuring a reunion of the original band, alongside a Sensible-augmented version of the *Phantasmagoria/Anything* line-up – playing a set of older classics, with not a hint of any more-recent major-label material. Devotees of the *Not of This Earth* era will love *Molten Lager* (1999, Musical Tragedies/Sudden Death): a 1994 recording, with the new songs sounding 'slightly' better in the live setting, and – to give credit where it's due – pretty good renditions of classics like 'Gun Fury' and 'Love Song'.

Once we get into the post-*Grave Disorder* era, the live releases come thick and fast, with a new live album or DVD/CD package cropping up seemingly every couple of years. These are generally excellent, highly professional performances, recorded very well; although, aside from changes of bassist, and minor setlist variations, there is relatively little to differentiate the albums. Though perhaps not necessarily essential, they're all worth a listen. *Tiki Nightmare – Live in London, 2002* – initially released as a DVD/CD pack by Union Square Pictures in 2003, later reissued through Let Them Eat Vinyl as an album in its own right – captures the *Grave Disorder* tour, with some selections from that album, plus a rare run-through of 'Street Of Dreams' from *Phantasmagoria*.

The *Machine Gun Etiquette Anniversary Live Set* (Easy Action, 2011) – another CD/DVD set – captures the Stu West line-up powering through highlights of that album at Manchester Academy, along with a selection of old faves, including the extended medley of 'Neat Neat Neat' and the Doors' 'Break On Through' that was a set lynchpin at the time.

The double CD *35th Anniversary Live in Concert* finds the band performing (almost) complete renditions of both *Damned Damned Damned* and *The Black Album*, at London's Roundhouse, the only track omitted being 'Stab Yor Back': presumably due to the ongoing feud between Rat and the Captain (For further insight, see Wes Orshoski's excellent documentary, *The Damned: Don't You Wish That We Were Dead* (2015)). The idea of 'legacy concerts' in which bands play their classic albums in full, is a popular one, although one could argue that only the most fanatical latter-day Damned devotee would be likely to spend much time listening to an album of the 2011 line-up performing *Damned Damned Damned* or *The Black Album*, when they could simply play the original records.

Another Live Album From the Damned (Let Them Eat Vinyl, 2014) is taken from the 2010 tour, and has a rather more interesting and varied track listing than most of their more recent live releases: featuring tracks from *Grave Disorder, So Who's Paranoid?* and more.

Finally, *40th Anniversary Tour – Live in Margate* (Live Here Now, 2017) is a sprawling triple LP, with more interesting set-list choices, ending with four songs recorded in soundcheck, including the underrated late-career classic, 'Under The Wheels'. As I say, casual fans aren't likely to require 'all' of these, but they each have their own merits, should you feel like investigating.

As a closing note, I must mention The Damned's post-*Evil Spirits* activity. While the recording schedule has generally been relaxed in the 21st century, the band's renewed commercial success in 2018 seems to have inspired a new sense of purpose. The 2019 *Black Is the Night* anthology peaked at number 63 in the UK: not bad considering the baffling array of Damned compilations already available. At the same time, the band headed back to their early-1980s haunt, Rockfield Studios, with producer Tom Dalgety: known for his work with Royal Blood, Rammstein and The Pixies, among many others. In 2020, the results of these sessions emerged as a new EP, titled *The Rockfield Files*: the band's second release since Paul Gray rejoined, and sadly, their last with Pinch, who amicably stepped down at the end of 2019, having completed an impressive twenty-year stint. The four songs retain elements of the *Evil Spirits* sound but have a harder, more guitar-heavy attack, which no doubt pleased Sensible, no end! 'Keep 'Em Alive' was released in advance of the EP, with a promo video combining live band clips with dizzying psychedelic countryside drone footage. The song addresses the vital role that bees play in our ecosystem via some punchy, anthemic pop-punk.

The next track, 'Manipulator', is one of the fiercest Damned songs recorded since the Captain's return. It recalls the drive and aggression of 'Ignite' or 'Machine Gun Etiquette', with Gray's magnificent, domineering bass, and Sensible's slashing, garage-punk guitar. Side two begins with 'The Spider & The Fly', which allows Vanian to inject the haunting piano intro with his customary Gothic mystique, before building to some catchy 1960s-inspired power pop containing strong hints of The Who and The Jimi Hendrix Experience.

The record concludes with the full version of 'Black Is the Night': an abridged version of which had appeared on the 2019 compilation of the same name. It's a wonderful vehicle for Vanian: a svelte mid-tempo baroque pop masterclass, reminiscent of John Barry's James Bond themes, with a breathtaking chorus, perfectly encapsulating The Damned's more dramatic, theatrical side; and even manages to squeeze in a reference to Pink Floyd's Barrett-era magnum opus, 'Interstellar Overdrive'.

Overall, *The Rockfield Files* is a fantastic EP, providing a bite-size overview of the things that make The Damned great. It was well-received, with fans responding enthusiastically and healthy sales taking it number 1 in the UK vinyl singles chart on the week of its release in October 2020. At the same time, rumours began to circulate that more exciting news was due from the Damned camp. The band's drum stool had been empty since late 2019, and interviews with Rat Scabies seemed to suggest he might be open to returning to the band, at least on a temporary basis. He and Gray had already reconciled their differences, and the two were playing together in The Professor and the Madman, alongside members of Orange County punk perennials, The Adolescent and D.I. Interviews with Vanian around this time. remained sceptical on the subject, with Vanian telling *Uncut* magazine that the chances of Rat rejoining were 'slim' due to ongoing personality clashes between Scabies and Sensible dating back to a dispute over royalty payments from the band's debut album.

Nevertheless, on 21 October – just five days after the release of *The Rockfield Files* – a press conference was held to announce a 45th-anniversary tour for 2021 (later postponed until the following year): with not just Rat, but also Brian James, returning to the fold; the full original line-up reuniting for what we are informed will be the final time, revisiting material from the first two albums. But we shouldn't take this as an indication that The Damned have finally succumbed to the temptations of a career in nostalgia. Sensible has indicated that the current line-up had been actively writing new material during the Covid-19 lockdown, and *The Rockfield Files* certainly seems to suggest that the Captain, Dave, Paul and Monty (and whoever ends up playing drums) still have a real creative drive which would not be satisfied by simply rehashing *Damned Damned Damned* over and over again. Whatever the future holds, it seems likely that Britain's greatest surviving punk band still have some surprises in store for us!

On Track series

Barclay James Harvest – Keith and Monica Domone 978-1-78952-067-5

The Beatles – Andrew Wild 978-1-78952-009-5

The Beatles Solo 1969-1980 – Andrew Wild 978-1-78952-030-9

Blue Oyster Cult – Jacob Holm-Lupo 978-1-78952-007-1

Kate Bush – Bill Thomas 978-1-78952-097-2

The Clash – Nick Assirati 978-1-78952-077-4

Crosby, Stills and Nash – Andrew Wild 978-1-78952-039-2

Deep Purple and Rainbow 1968-79 – Steve Pilkington 978-1-78952-002-6

Dire Straits – Andrew Wild 978-1-78952-044-6

Dream Theater – Jordan Blum 978-1-78952-050-7

Emerson Lake and Palmer – Mike Goode 978-1-78952-000-2

Fairport Convention – Kevan Furbank 978-1-78952-051-4

Genesis – Stuart MacFarlane 978-1-78952-005-7

Gentle Giant – Gary Steel 978-1-78952-058-3

Hawkwind – Duncan Harris 978-1-78952-052-1

Iron Maiden – Steve Pilkington 978-1-78952-061-3

Jethro Tull – Jordan Blum 978-1-78952-016-3

Elton John in the 1970s – Peter Kearns 978-1-78952-034-7

Gong – Kevan Furbank 978-1-78952-082-8

Iron Maiden – Steve Pilkington 978-1-78952-061-3

Judas Priest – John Tucker 978-1-78952-018-7

Kansas – Kevin Cummings 978-1-78952-057-6

Aimee Mann – Jez Rowden 978-1-78952-036-1

Joni Mitchell – Peter Kearns 978-1-78952-081-1

The Moody Blues – Geoffrey Feakes 978-1-78952-042-2

Mike Oldfield – Ryan Yard 978-1-78952-060-6

Queen – Andrew Wild 978-1-78952-003-3

Renaissance – David Detmer 978-1-78952-062-0

The Rolling Stones 1963-80 – Steve Pilkington 978-1-78952-017-0

Steely Dan – Jez Rowden 978-1-78952-043-9

Thin Lizzy – Graeme Stroud 978-1-78952-064-4

Toto – Jacob Holm-Lupo 978-1-78952-019-4

U2 – Eoghan Lyng 978-1-78952-078-1

UFO – Richard James 978-1-78952-073-6

The Who – Geoffrey Feakes 978-1-78952-076-7

Roy Wood and the Move – James R Turner 978-1-78952-008-8

Van Der Graaf Generator – Dan Coffey 978-1-78952-031-6

Yes – Stephen Lambe 978-1-78952-001-9

Frank Zappa 1966 to 1979 – Eric Benac 978-1-78952-033-0

10CC – Peter Kearns 978-1-78952-054-5

Decades Series

Pink Floyd In The 1970s – Georg Purvis 978-1-78952-072-9

Marillion in the 1980s – Nathaniel Webb 978-1-78952-065-1

On Screen series

Carry On... – Stephen Lambe 978-1-78952-004-0

David Cronenberg – Patrick Chapman 978-1-78952-071-2

Doctor Who: The David Tennant Years – Jamie Hailstone 978-1-78952-066-8

Monty Python – Steve Pilkington 978-1-78952-047-7

Seinfeld Seasons 1 to 5 – Stephen Lambe 978-1-78952-012-5

Other Books

Derek Taylor: For Your Radioactive Children – Andrew Darlington 978-1-78952-

Jon Anderson and the Warriors - the road to Yes – David Watkinson 978-1-78952-059-0

Tommy Bolin: In and Out of Deep Purple – Laura Shenton 978-1-78952-070-5

Maximum Darkness – Deke Leonard 978-1-78952-048-4

Maybe I Should've Stayed In Bed – Deke Leonard 978-1-78952-053-8

The Twang Dynasty – Deke Leonard 978-1-78952-049-1

and many more to come!